BERT MONROY

PHOTOREALISTIC TECHNIQUES WITH PHOTOSHOP & ILLUSTRATOR

by bert monroy

New Riders

201 West 103rd Street, Indianapolis, Indiana 46290

Bert Monroy:
Photorealistic Techniques with Photoshop & Illustrator

International Standard Book Number: 0-7357-0969-6

Library of Congress Catalog Card Number: 99-067434

Printed in the United States of America

First Printing: December 1999

03 02 01 00 99   7 6 5 4 3 2 1

Interpretation of the printing code: The rightmost double-digit number is the year of the book's printing; the rightmost single-digit number is the number of the book's printing. For example, the printing code 99-1 shows that the first printing of the book occurred in 1999.

Trademarks

Warning and Disclaimer

Publisher
David Dwyer

Executive Editor
Steve Weiss

Development Editor
Barb Terry

Managing Editor
Jennifer Eberhardt

Copy Editor
Gail S. Burlakoff

Indexer
Tim Wright

Technical Reviewer
Luanne Cohen

Production
Kim Scott
www.bumpy.com

Proofreaders
Sheri Replin
Nancy Sixsmith

Cover Design
Aren Howell

Book Design
Louisa Klucznik

Foreword

by Russell Preston Brown

Like I always say: A detailed analysis of the details, in the detail, is detailed in the details. I know it sounds like I'm crazy. (By the way, I am.) The point I'm trying to make is that the beauty of art and design is truly in the details of the final piece.

We seem to be able to dream up a good idea, but getting it to look real is another thing. Can you tell me the color of the shadow that your blue car casts on your driveway? Do you know what typefaces are used on all the signs you see on your way to work? Can you have a shadow on a shadow?

If you've never asked yourself some of these questions as you're working on an illustration in Adobe Photoshop or Adobe Illustrator, then STOP what you're doing and read this book!

In this eye-opening book, Bert Monroy takes you on a guided tour of the art of observation. He teaches you that observing the little things around you is a critical part of making things look realistic. Beware! In the process of reading this book, Mr. Monroy will open your eyes, shake your brain, and reconnect your head to your body. It may hurt a bit, but it will be well worth it. This is the kind of book that everyone needs now and again, to clear one's mind and start *looking*, instead of just walking around on autopilot. Start noticing the subtleties in life and make your illustrations look a hundred times better—that's what this book is all about.

Russell Preston Brown
Sr. Creative Director Adobe Systems Inc.

Foreword

by Diane Fenster

Bert's work has always intrigued me. For years I have been trying to figure out exactly what it is in his work that seems to go beyond the boundaries of what I normally think of as photorealism. I've looked at how he uses color, how he arranges detail, and how he juxtaposes complex shapes and simple forms; and I think that they all work together to form a kind of magic realism that shimmers with a dynamic tension beyond what we consider to be ordinary reality.

In reviewing the techniques and methods Bert presents in this wonderful book, I realized that my initial impressions were correct. The magic lies in the unity of all these artistic concerns. I was struck by the incredible details of the urban scapes he presents as examples and how they reflect both the microcosm and macrocosm of the viewer's reality. No matter where your eye stops, complex forms have been reduced to simple color and shape, reconstructed and put back together into a "painted" world that reflects this new reality, a reality that moves beyond "photo" to where paint and draftsmanship collide. Whether you zoom in on the headlines of a newspaper in the newsstand or pan back to the perspective of the entire building on the corner, it doesn't seem to matter... everywhere there is a rich visual feast for the viewer.

For the reader of this book, your artistic task is to take the encyclopedic array of information presented here as technique and methodology and reconstruct from it your own world. I think this is the responsibility that Bert leaves you. As in all classical instruction, the student is taught the techniques of how to formally move beyond what the teacher has presented as examples. The next generation of digital artist will be able to pull this book from their library and point to it as a place where they began their artistic journey.

Bravo Bert!

Diane Fenster
Photo/Illustrator

Foreword

by Jeff Schewe

When I first saw Bert's work, two distinct aspects struck me: his sense of vision and his convincing, photo-realistic painting. Oh, there was something else about his work—I knew he must be a frigging maniac. His work is super-realistic, and I know what that kind of realism requires—fanatic attention to detail. Bert does details really well! He still calls himself a painter, but his pigments are made of pixels.

In any kind of true art, there is both craft and vision. The craft part can be learned. The vision thing is something that must evolve. In this book, Bert shares both his craft AND his vision. Anybody who wants to learn the craft of drawing and painting on the computer should read this book. But it doesn't end there. Bert also generously shares his reasons for doing what he does: his vision. And that is priceless.

Jeff Schewe
Photographer/Imaging Artist

Contents at a Glance

Images at a Glance

Table of Contents

About the Author

Bert Monroy is an Illustrator and a photorealistic painter. He was born and raised in New York City where he spent 20 years in the advertising industry as an art director and creative director for various agencies, as well as his own.

Upon discovering computers with the introduction of the Macintosh 128 in 1984, he embarked on a new digital career. He embraced the computer as an artistic medium and is considered one of the pioneers of digital art. Bert's work has been seen in every major publication. His work has also been featured in scores of books, including *Making Art on a Macintosh, The Photoshop WOW Book* (all editions), *The Illustrator WOW Book* (all editions), *The Art of Digital Painting, The Grey Book,* and *The Photoshop A to Z* in Japan. His work was also used to introduce many software products such as VideoWorks, PixelPaint, SoundCap and ImageStudio.

Bert was a founding partner in the New York firm Incredible Interactivity, which was responsible for interactive multimedia presentations as early as 1986 before the terms had even been coined. He has created presentations for such clients as General Motors, American Express, and Knoll International.

Bert co-authored *The Official Adobe Photoshop Handbook*, the first book on Photoshop and the only one on the market for over a year. It won various awards. He co-authored *Adobe Photoshop: A Visual Guide to the Mac* (published in six languages and published in the United States by Addison-Wesley), and *Photoshop 4,* (published in Japan by Agosto and BNN). Bert co-authored the book *Photoshop Channel Chops* with David Biedny and Nathan Moody, a book that concentrates on the most advanced features of the program not covered anywhere else.

Bert is an accomplished teacher and lecturer who has served on the faculties of The School of Visual Arts (NYC), Center for Creative Imaging (ME), Dynamic Graphics Educational Foundation (IL), and California College of Arts & Crafts (CA). He lectures at many other institutions around the world and currently teaches at San Francisco State University.

In 1993, Bert moved his studio from New York City to Berkeley, California. He continues to serve his installed base of clients which include Apple Computer, Adobe Systems, Pioneer Electronics, Fujitsu, SONY, AT&T, Chevron, and American Express. He has appeared as a regular guest on the television programs *Digital Gurus, MacTV,* and many other technology and art TV shows in Japan. Bert has also done a considerable amount of film work for Industrial Light & Magic, Pacific Data Images. and R/Greenberg Assoc. He recently worked with IDIG in creating many of the effects for the movie "SPAWN."

Acknowledgments

There are so many people I wish to thank that I almost need to publish a separate book. It's like those acceptance speeches at the Academy Awards—I could go on forever. But seriously, some people must be mentioned.

There's a great bunch of folks at New Riders that deserve tremendous appreciation for an outstanding job. I have done many books before, but this was the first without a hitch. Thanks go to Chris Nelson, who started the ball rolling and is a generally cool guy, and to Steve Weiss, who picked up the ball and ran with it to the goal line. Special thanks to Jennifer Eberhardt and Barb Terry, who kept me on schedule and took care of things. To the copy editor, Gail S. Burlakoff, the design team, and all the rest of the NRP folks, my heartfelt thanks.

My wife Zosia deserves a big hand for putting up with my long hours. She also met the deadlines I imposed on her as my first-line-of-defense proofreader. She got the first draft that came right from my head and fingers and helped ensure that it made sense.

Big thanks to Luanne Cohen; her suggestions early on helped me to organize the flow of the book.

Now come the personal thanks:

David Biedny who has co-authored so many books with me and sold me my first computer back in 1984. A friend and an inspiration for a long time, he has always pushed me to do better than I thought I could. Thanks, dude.

Thanks to Don Ross, the first person to push me to write. "Write how you speak," he said. Of course, that's why I need my wife to proof things.

My high school buddy, John Melo—if it weren't for him, I never would have pursued a career in art.

Sister St. Helen, who convinced me to go to the High School of Art & Design in New York City, instead of the school I was about to enter. She was definitely trying to tell me something.

John and Tom Knoll, for dreaming up Photoshop and making it happen.

Thanks to the folks at Adobe, for picking up where John and Tom left off. I also want to thank them for putting out so many other great software packages. In this group, special thanks go to Mark Hamburg and Chris Cox. Also part of this group, but with added features, are Russell Brown and his wife Jan.

The folks at Apple, for putting out a machine that got me hooked into this stuff in the first place. My studio is still surrounded by Apple logos.

My kids, Sean and Erika—even though they are grown and on their own, they still keep me grounded in reality.

My Mother—if it weren't for her, this book would be blank.

My sisters, Diana and Irene, because they're cool. Diana's husband, Richie, and her son, Joey, for the same reason.

My good friend Bill Schoenberg, for those Friday afternoon hikes that gave me the badly needed break from the grind.

My other nephew, Mark, and his roomy, Frank, for all the diversions. Mark's brother, Chris, because he's Chris—and their mother, Iza, because she's Iza.

Since I entered the digital realm, I have had the immense pleasure of meeting many wonderful people, all of whom need to be thanked for something or other. I can't name them all, so if I missed you here, don't sweat it—you're in my heart: Cathy Abes; Bren Anderson; Bill Atkinson; Bob Bowen; Tony Bove and Cheryl Rhodes and the boys; Matt Brown; Casey; Sandee Cohen; Frank Colin; Linnea Dayton; Jack Davis; John Dvorak; Mark Drury; Katrin Eisman; Travis Estrella; Etsuro Endo; Susumo Endo; Chuck Farnham; Diane Fenster and Miles; Glenn Fisher; Michael Gosney; Thea Grigsby and her husband Steven; Steve Guttman and Jenny and the kids; Michael Hanes; Jerry Harris and family; Tom Hedges; Helene; Ichiro Hirose and family; George Jardine;

Yoshinori Kaizu; Kenn Krasner; Bob Levitus; the Linde brothers, Peter and Bruce; Ray Lonsdale; Jim Ludtke and Sharon; Keith Macgreggor and family; Chris Mains; Paul Mavrides; Deke McClellan; Steve Mitchell and Judy; Nathan Moody; Stanley Mouse; Carl Munoz; the Neal brothers, Brad and Tom; Barbara Nessim; Mark Newhouse; Walter Obrien; Cher Pendarvis and Steve; Howard Penner; Carol Person; Ron Rick and family; Tom Rielly; Paul Rosenfeld; Nancy Ruenzel; Todd Rundgren and his wife Michelle; David Schargel; Stuart Sharpe and family; Russell Sparkman and family; Sharon Steuer and Jeff; Tamara Street; Fran Stiles; Will and Rebecca Tate; Robin Williams and family; Colin Wood; Mark Wood, and Becky and the girls; Mark Zimmer; everybody that was at CCI; everybody at the School of Visual Arts. Man, there are so many more, but I have gone over my page count. Love ya all!

Just one more thing: I want to thank all my students and the attendees of my seminars for all the ooohs and aahhhs that make the job so much fun.

A Message from New Riders

Welcome to the Digital Masters series.

New Riders has traditionally focused its graphics publishing eye on tools and techniques, but this is the first time we've dedicated a book encompassing tools and techniques to the vision of a single artist. We recognized that a rare few artists have a pretty cool combination of

1. an absolute mastery of their medium

2. an amazing ability to teach and to bring out the best in those who study with them.

And we wanted to give the ever-growing number of artists—commercial and creative—who have dedicated themselves to mastering digital media a chance to learn not only about tools and techniques, but also about how the masters pull it all together to craft their creations. If you could just sit down with some of these masters and get in their heads for a little while, see what

they're seeing and hear their reasoning as to how a piece is conceived and executed, and if you could apply what you learned to your own situation, imagine the places you could go...

That's what we've tried to do with Digital Masters. Think of this as the souvenir program-cum-notebook you take away from your own personal seminar with a master artist.

Which brings us to Bert Monroy, who'd probably prefer that we not go endlessly singing his praises and that we'd let his work—the rest of this book—speak for itself. Fair enough. Bert tends to earn the instant respect of everyone who interacts with him, and this project has been no exception. He's simply one of the best you'll ever see at doing photorealistic digital art; and he's one of the best authors we've ever had the pleasure of partnering with.

To Bert: Thanks, man. The pleasure's been all ours.

To Bert's readers and students: We hope this book works for you. Let us know.

How to Contact Us

As the reader of this book, *you* are our most important critic and commentator. We value your opinion and want to know what we're doing right, what we could do better, in what areas you'd like to see us publish, and any other words of wisdom you're willing to pass our way.

As the Executive Editor for the Graphics team at New Riders, I welcome your comments. You can fax, email, or write me directly to let me know what you did or didn't like about this book—as well as what we can do to make our books better.

Please note that I cannot help you with technical problems related to the topic of this book, and that due to the high volume of mail I receive, I might not be able to reply to every message.

When you write, please be sure to include this book's title, ISBN, and author, as well as your name and phone or fax number. I will carefully review your comments and share them with the authors and editors who worked on the book.

For any issues directly related to this or other titles:

Email: steve.weiss@newriders.com

Mail: Steve Weiss
          Executive Editor
          Professional Graphics & Design Publishing
          New Riders Publishing
          201 West 103rd Street
          Indianapolis, IN 46290 USA

Visit Our Website: www.newriders.com

On our website you'll find information about our other books, the authors we partner with, book updates and file downloads, promotions, discussion boards for online interaction with other users and with technology experts, and a calendar of trade shows and other professional events with which we'll be involved. We hope to see you around.

Email Us from Our Website

Go to www.newriders.com and click on the Contact link if you

- Have comments or questions about this book

- Want to report errors that you have found in this book

- Have a book proposal or are otherwise interested in writing with New Riders

- Would like us to send you one of our author kits

- Are an expert in a computer topic or technology and are interested in being a reviewer or technical editor

- Want to find a distributor for our titles in your area

- Are an educator/instructor who wishes to preview New Riders books for classroom use. (Include your name, school, department, address, phone number, office days/hours, text currently in use, and enrollment in your department in the body/comments area, along with your request for desk/examination copies, or for additional information.

Call Us or Fax Us

You can reach us toll-free at (800) 571-5840 + 9 + 3567. Ask for New Riders.

If outside the USA, please call 1-317-581-3500. Ask for New Riders.

If you prefer, you can fax us at 317-581-4663, Attention: New Riders.

Introduction

A good friend and fellow artist recently said to me, "You're crazy for writing this book. You're giving away all your secrets." I gave it a lot of thought. Are they my secrets? Or are they techniques I have developed over time? I don't feel I am giving them away. I am sharing them. I am a teacher, and teachers share the things they have mastered with their students. Besides, I didn't give everything away. The book is too short for that.

My goal with this book is to give you a better understanding of the methods I use to create the images I paint. I don't expect you to suddenly become a photorealist painter or illustrator. Rather, I hope that you will take these techniques and mix them with your own creative juices to express your own art.

The way I see it, I can't imagine everyone buying a set of water-colors or oil paints, but many people do own Photoshop. Photoshop has become crucial tool in many business environments. Many scanners include the software, and we are bombarded by images done in Photoshop on the Web, in junk mail and magazines—anywhere there is a visual. So people have the tools, but having the tools does not make them artists.

I once taught a class on advanced digital illustration and gave the class an assignment that required painting from life. One of the students was obviously having a very difficult time with the project. When I asked her what was wrong, she said she didn't know how to draw. I asked her what she did at her job. She was a filing clerk. "Why was a company spending money to send a filing clerk to an advanced illustration class?" I asked. She told me that the bosses wanted her to learn the Mac so they could fire the art director and have her do his job. I think this mode of thinking is similar to one of the hurdles digital art has come up against: "The computer does all the work—all you need is a body sitting in front of it to push the buttons."

It took some time for Photography to become recognized as an art form. The thought was that "anybody can take a picture." It wasn't long before we realized that not everybody has the eye of an Ansel Adams.

The computer is a tool. Give someone on the street a full set of oil paints and all the canvas they could ever use, and chances are you'll get nothing back. Give an artist a piece of charcoal and see what you get.

Not everyone is born with an "artistic talent." However, many of us *are* born with the innate talent but lack the formal training to do anything with it. That is what I hope to accomplish with this book: Not formal training perhaps, but a starting point from which to explore. A look into what it takes to, say, draw a little tree.

I have been drawing since I can remember. My mother still has a drawing I did when I was two years old. And if I had a penny for every time I was scolded at school for drawing, I would be very well off right now. I am lucky. Now I get paid to draw. I am an illustrator. However, this book deals with a very small portion of my commercial work. The main focus of the book is on the other aspect of my work—my fine art.

The pages of this book are filled with my art, with what I do for my own creative fulfillment. The techniques I develop in the course of creating one of my paintings, I then apply to my commercial work. These are the techniques I share with you.

My paintings are a very personal treasure to me. They might not be what other people want to hang over their couch, but that is not my goal in creating them. I paint scenes that mean something to me. Many of them have jumped out at me as I passed them on the street. Many of my subjects are worn, decaying buildings. They seem to tell so many stories. They have seen so much, yet no one seems to care what stories they can tell. In painting the building, I try to capture the souls that haunt them. I show them devoid of people because people would intrude on their solitude.

I grew up in New York City, and solitude was something I found in my paintings. It gave me a way to communicate with my surroundings in a personal way. After I was transplanted to California, my focus changed and now includes more natural settings. These images are also devoid of humans in order to let the spirits that inhabit them speak freely.

In sharing my paintings with you and others, it is my hope that you will stop for a minute and look around. Take a deep breath and leave all other distractions aside. Just share the silence and serenity of something as mundane as a store window.

I have heard the question "Why don't you just take a photograph?" a million times. Well, for one thing, I'm not a photographer. To me, it is the journey, not the end result, that is important. When I start a painting, I am filled with excitement—an excitement that grows with each new development and that comes to an end when the piece is completed. At that point, I can't wait to start the next one.

Before the computer came into my life, my paintings were similar in style and content to what they are today. They just took a lot longer to produce. Many times a spill of paint meant starting all over again. (If only life had an "Undo" feature.)

With the computer, the creative process flows unabated. The medium becomes transparent. For me, the computer is the preferred medium. I paint what I see; therefore, painting with light is the perfect technique for me.

Since I will be giving you my "secrets," let's make it personal. I would like to invite you into my studio. I work at home, but my studio is not technically "in my house." I like to tell people that I commute to work and that I walk all the way. It's a distance of only about 65 feet, but it's still a walk.

I moved to the Bay Area in 1993. I now live in the Berkeley Hills. From my patio, a path leads up to my studio (Figure 1).

1 My studio is located in a small building behind my house. A small path leads up to it and passes by a couple of redwood trees.

2 This is the side of my studio where I do my work. I am surrounded by humming machines that allow me to explore a world of dreams. Oh yeah, and get some work done.

The interior of my studio is quiet, a far cry from growing up next to the BQE in Brooklyn, New York. In Figure 2, you can see the side of the studio where I spend a major portion of my life. There are many machines around me because painting isn't all I do with computers. I also create multimedia presentations and 3D works that require a lot of computer power. It is at those terminals that I have developed many of the techniques you will learn in this book.

The other side of the studio holds my wife's work station, printers, bookcases—the usual stuff that goes into a studio.

Giving away my secrets? I don't expect a sudden flood of photo-realistic work to saturate the market. I do hope to give you that little bit of knowledge and skill that will let your wildest dreams come to life. Have fun...that's what it's really all about.

–Bert Monroy

chapter 1

Starting with the Basics

Before we enter the book, I want to introduce a few software features that you may not be totally aware of. These features are referred to extensively throughout the book, and I want to make clear what they are.

In this first chapter, I also show you the procedures I follow to prepare elements for my paintings.

Software Features

The process for creating an image varies according to what I intend to accomplish. The computer has made it very easy for the artist to wear many hats. The computer makes it possible to be a sculptor, photographer, painter, video and film editor, sound producer, and special effects artist and gives you access to many additional graphic arts skills—all without having to leave your chair.

Photoshop Layers

Layers are part of an image. A Photoshop document can have up to 99 layers present in each file. Each of these layers can contain elements of the overall image. Only the Photoshop format can contain layers; it is the only format available when you save a file that has layers.

In Photoshop, the

layers can be

manipulated in as

many ways as you

want, without

affecting the rest

of the image.

Fortunately, other programs can recognize a layered Photoshop document. A great example is Adobe After Effects, which imports Photoshop files with the individual layers intact. You can then apply effects and animate each layer separately from the others.

In Photoshop, the layers can be manipulated in as many ways as you want, without affecting the rest of the image. Photoshop layers have many functions that I do not discuss in this book because it is limited to a set number of pages. Many other books are available where you can find out more about layers. And don't forget the manual that comes with Photoshop.

Layer Masks

I do want to touch on a few aspects of layers, however, as they will appear throughout the book. One is the *layer mask,* which is applied to a layer to allow portions of the layer to be seen.

In the layer mask, you apply tones from white to black, with 254 additional grays in between. Where the mask is white, you can see the contents of that layer. Where the mask is black, the contents of the layer are hidden. Likewise, the level of gray in between will determine the level of visibility of that area of the layer. For example, a 50 percent gray will make the layer 50 percent visible.

Other aspects of layers are presented at different points throughout the book. I have placed these bits of information where they are pertinent.

The Alpha Channel

Another feature I mention many times throughout the book is the *alpha channel.* This feature of Photoshop is extremely important—so much so that I co-authored, with David Biedny and Nathan Moody, a book dedicated primarily to this very subject. That book is *Photoshop Channel Chops* from New Riders, the publisher of this book. *Chops* stands for channel operations.

I want to give you a brief introduction to the concept of the alpha channel and how it relates to the creation of my paintings.

Unlike the layer, the alpha channel is not part of the image. It is part of the *file,* in that the various alpha channels are saved with the file. But they are not seen as part of the image.

The alpha channels are masks through which you can apply effects. The way they work is similar to the way a layer mask works. They both use white to black, with gray in between.

In the layer mask, the tones determine what will be seen and what won't. The alpha channel uses the tones to expose the image to an effect. Alpha channels are basically specialized selection processes.

When you use the selection tools, you are segregating a portion of the image to be modified. The actual selection process does nothing to the image. It's the application of a filter, adjustment control, or any other modification through that selection that will affect the image. This is the same concept behind the alpha channel. It is merely a selection to expose the image for an effect to be applied.

The beauty of these alpha channels is that they can be saved and modified. When you use the Lasso, you make a selection. When you deselect, the selection is gone. If you choose Save Selection (Select>Save Selection), the selection is sent to an alpha channel that can be recalled as many times as necessary.

You can paint right in the alpha channel with any of the tools, and you can also use filters in alpha channels. This opens the door to many possible effects, many of which will be explored in this book.

You can have 24 channels present in a Photoshop file. The color space uses some of the channels—RGB takes up three channels (Red, Green, and Blue), for example, leaving 21 channels for you to use as alpha channels. When you choose Save Selection, you have the option of sending the selection to a new document. This option sends the selection to a separate file that you can access when you choose Load Selection (Select>Load Selection) to call up an alpha channel. Saving selections gives you the capability to have thousands of alpha channels.

Throughout the book, I will refer many times to alpha channels. Now I hope you have a basic understanding of what they are.

You can paste Illustrator files into a

Photoshop file as either pixels or paths.

The Illustrator/Photoshop Connection

In Illustrator, I create the basic elements for an image. The fact that I can work large and reduce the image without any loss of detail is very important. When Illustrator files are imported into a Photoshop file, they are rasterized to the resolution of the Photoshop document: Any colors and stroke weight added to shapes in Illustrator will be converted to shapes and strokes with those attributes in the Photoshop file. The dimensions of the shapes will be identical in both programs. The *rasterization* is the number of pixels assigned to the shapes once they enter Photoshop. Illustrator does give you the capability to set resolution for its files. In the case of exporting to a Photoshop file, this resolution setting is not necessary.

An inch will still be an inch. The number of pixels in that inch is determined by the resolution set in the Photoshop file. If the object in Illustrator measures four-by-six inches, it will measure four-by-six inches in the Photoshop file. If the resolution of the Photoshop file is set to 72 pixels to an inch, the element imported from Illustrator will measure 284-by-432 pixels. When the resolution of the Photoshop file is set to 300 pixels to an inch, the element imported from Illustrator measures 1200-by-1800 pixels. The numbers are simply the inches multiplied by the pixels per inch.

You can paste Illustrator files into a Photoshop file as either pixels or paths. I import them as pixels if I have assigned the desired attributes to shapes created in Illustrator. In the course of the book, I demonstrate several times where I have done this and why.

Sometimes I import the Illustrator files as paths. When the files are imported into Photoshop, they appear in the Path palette. The imported path becomes a *Work Path*, a temporary path that you must save if you want to use it more than once. In these cases, I assign color, texture, or any other desired attribute in Photoshop. The path becomes the method for selecting areas for colorization and so on.

In the Beginning...

Here I sit in front of a blank screen. Ready to begin. I have a feeling of anticipation that was lacking when I sat before a blank canvas. The possibilities are so much greater in the digital world. The mere fact of being able to select a color immediately lets the creative flow take me wherever I want. No time wasted mixing colors to get just that perfect blue for the sky.

Where do I start? Adobe Illustrator is usually the first program I open. Adobe Illustrator has become my sketching tool. When the program made its debut, I fell in love with the ability to bend lines to create shapes. I had been a fan of French curves for many years, and now I was presented with a digital tool that took that concept far beyond anything I ever dreamed of.

Usually an image starts out as a sketch. The sketch can be a pencil drawing that is then scanned into the computer. Or the sketch can be outlined by computer from the start.

Illustrator is like the pencil on the canvas that I used in traditional media. The flexibility, coupled with the low RAM usage, makes it the ideal tool for clicking away to my heart's content.

Let me begin by showing you the process I use to deal with my commercial illustrations.

The Idea Stage

Figure 1 is a sketch that was faxed to me by a client. He had made some pencil roughs on a legal pad (note the lines of the paper). The concept was for a program for telecommunications. The client wanted the package to show a modem racing down a road as if it were a car.

I took the layout a step further and suggested that the actual boundary of the ad be lessened so that the modem/car could take up the open space and appear to be leaping out of the ad.

I created a layout sketch in Adobe Illustrator to show this new concept (Figure 2). Color was not necessary, since I intended to send this layout back to the client via fax. I made sure to choose a series of contrasting grays that would be readable on a fax.

After I received client approval, I took the same Illustrator file and imported it into Adobe Photoshop, where I completed the illustration (Figure 3). The paths present in the Illustrator file were imported into Photoshop as paths. Each of the paths was then used to select areas to be filled with color and texture.

1 The client faxed a rough layout giving direction for the creation of my illustration.

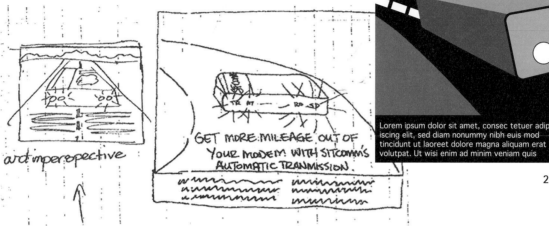

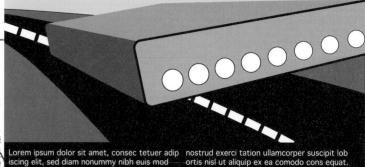

2 In Illustrator, I created a layout showing the proposed placement of the elements in the illustration. This was faxed to the client for approval.

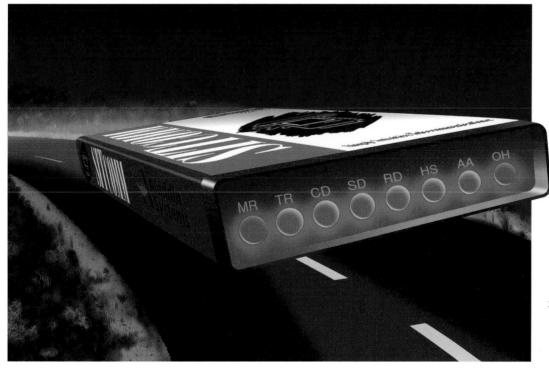

3 The Illustrator file became the basis for the final art. The paths were imported into Photoshop as paths, which were then turned into selections where color, detail, and texture were added.

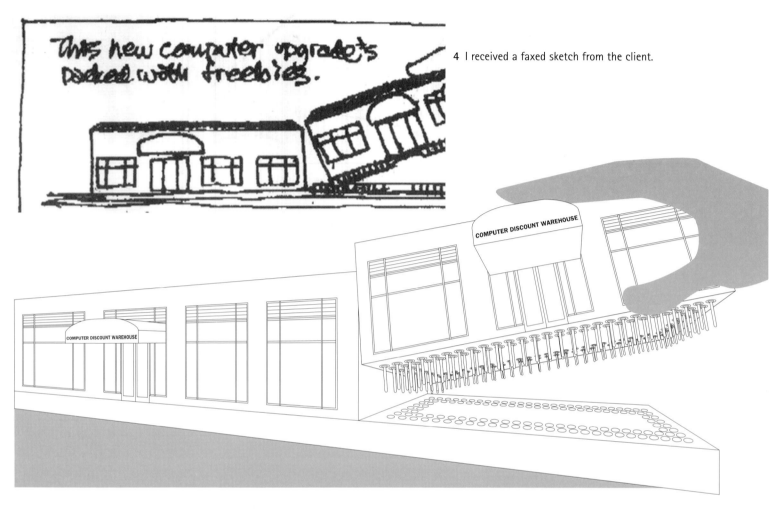

4 I received a faxed sketch from the client.

5 The layout was produced in Illustrator and was faxed back to the client for approval.

Figures 4, 5, and 6 show another example of the process of visualization. In this case, an ad agency needed art for a billboard. Their client was expanding by taking over a facility next door to their current site. The ad agency wanted to make it look as if the store was *upgrading* (as in computer terminology).

The client faxed me a rough sketch of the general concept (Figure 4). I added a little perspective, to make it easier to distinguish the pins and socket of the computer-type upgrade. I also felt the added angles would give the image movement. When I was finished, I faxed my version back to the client for approval (Figure 5). Once the client gave their approval, I imported the paths from Illustrator into Photoshop for the creation of the final image (Figure 6).

6 The final illustration.

The Sketch

The layouts I send to the clients are very similar to the process I follow in the creation of my paintings. There is always a sketch. In the next chapter, we will explore the procedures I follow for these preliminary sketches that determine the placement of elements.

Now, however, I want to start to build up an image. At the beginning of this chapter, I compared the sketch in Illustrator to the traditional pencil outlines on canvas.

In Figure 7, we see one of these sketches. It is a series of simple lines, laid out in Adobe Illustrator. These lines will be used as a guide. They will give me markers for the placement of the elements that will become the final art. The lines are assigned a black stroke with enough weight so that they can be seen when they are imported into Photoshop.

7 These are the lines for the sketch of the painting *Pic-n-Pac*.

I copy these lines to the Clipboard, and then, in Photoshop, I paste them into the file. Photoshop gives you the option to paste them as pixels or as paths. These "sketch lines" are pasted as pixels, which means that the color and line weight assigned in Illustrator will now be rasterized to the resolution of the Photoshop file into which they are being pasted. When something is pasted into a Photoshop document, it is placed in its own layer. I name this layer "outline."

I lower the opacity of this "outline" layer so I can use it as a guide to build the painting underneath it. Figure 8 shows the painting in progress, with the outline as a translucent line.

8 The painting *Pic-n-Pac* is seen here in progress. The layer of the outline is visible as a soft guide over the painting.

Creating Basic Shapes

I also create the various elements of a painting first in Illustrator. This differs from the sketch in that these Illustrator files are actual elements of the painting. The ability to make easy modifications to a shape makes this a valuable starting point. This method of working has other advantages, too. It allows me to get details I cannot get working in the actual Photoshop file. Let's examine a few of these advantages and see how they apply to my paintings.

How does this process of sketching in one program and then using it as a guide work in real life? Well, take a look at the preliminary sketching for *Akihabara*, one of my illustrations.

The electronics district of Tokyo is an alluring Mecca for the fans of electronic technology. There are things found there that can't be seen anywhere else on the planet. The painting *Akihabara* is a storefront on a corner of this wonderfully chaotic district (Figure 9).

One major obstacle for me in this painting was the accuracy of the massive amount of text visible throughout the store. Unlike a similar scene on the streets of America, I couldn't fake the text with my own verbiage. I had no idea what all these symbols said. They had to be accurate.

The scene had some interesting letterforms and styles I needed to match. The majority of the symbols were colored shapes, outlined in white with an additional outline and depth in black.

9 Akihabara is a store on a corner of Tokyo's electronics district.

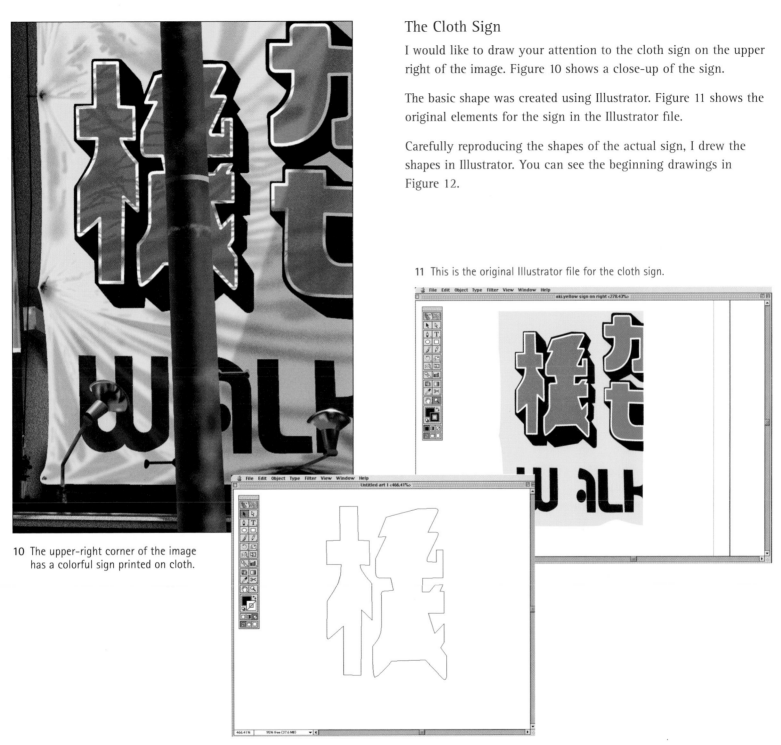

The Cloth Sign

I would like to draw your attention to the cloth sign on the upper right of the image. Figure 10 shows a close-up of the sign.

The basic shape was created using Illustrator. Figure 11 shows the original elements for the sign in the Illustrator file.

Carefully reproducing the shapes of the actual sign, I drew the shapes in Illustrator. You can see the beginning drawings in Figure 12.

11 This is the original Illustrator file for the cloth sign.

10 The upper-right corner of the image has a colorful sign printed on cloth.

12 The shapes for the characters were carefully reproduced.

The shapes were filled with a red color that closely matched the one on the actual signs (Figure 13). I do tend to exaggerate my colors.

All the paths were selected and copied to the Clipboard.

The existing, selected character shapes were given a thick white stroke (Figure 14).

The red letters, currently in the Clipboard, were pasted directly on top of the stroked ones. To ensure the proper positioning, I chose Edit>Paste In Front.

I pasted another copy in front and stroked it with black. This stroke was twice as thick as the white stroke. I then distorted portions of the characters to give this copy the 3D depth that the characters had in the sign (Figure 15).

Then I sent these black-stroked characters to the back of the other two (Object> Arrange>Send To Back). The result was a reproduction of the characters that appeared on the sign (Figure 16).

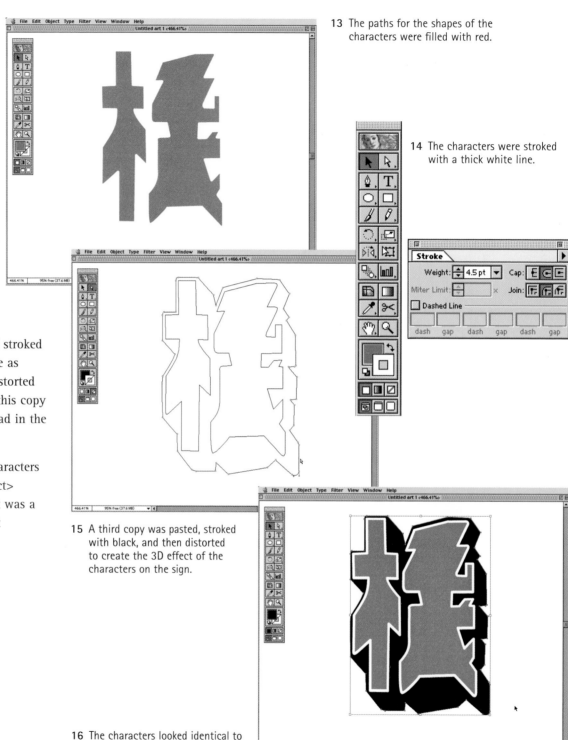

13 The paths for the shapes of the characters were filled with red.

14 The characters were stroked with a thick white line.

15 A third copy was pasted, stroked with black, and then distorted to create the 3D effect of the characters on the sign.

16 The characters looked identical to the ones on the actual sign.

17 When you paste objects from Illustrator into Photoshop via the Clipboard, you are given the choice of how they will be read.

I generated the other characters in the same way and saved the file. Then I selected all the objects in the file and copied them to the Clipboard.

In Photoshop, the contents of the Clipboard were pasted into the working document. The contents of the Clipboard were the paths from the Illustrator file. Photoshop gives you the option to paste them as pixels or paths (Figure 17).

As I mentioned before, when you paste as pixels, the shapes come into the Photoshop file and rasterize to the resolution of the file. Any color fills or colored strokes that were added in Illustrator will be present in the pasted element.

If you paste as paths, only the paths are pasted into the file. They appear as a Work Path in the Photoshop Paths palette. This Work Path contains all the paths that were selected and copied in the Illustrator file.

note | A Work Path is a temporary path. You must save it if you want to use it more than once. If you turn off the Work Path, any action you take with the Path tool replaces the contents of the previous Work Path with those of the new one being created.

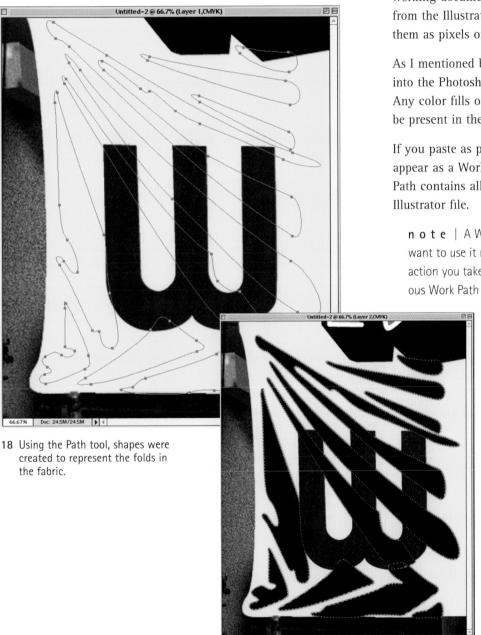

18 Using the Path tool, shapes were created to represent the folds in the fabric.

In this case, I pasted the Illustrator objects into the Photoshop file as pixels. The colored strokes and fills I created in Illustrator automatically fell into their own layer.

With the Photoshop Path tool, I created a series of shapes to represent the folds in the fabric (Figure 18).

These paths were turned into selections, with a small feather to soften the edges (Figure 19). A new layer was created to work in. The selected areas were then filled with black.

19 The Paths were turned into selections and filled with black in a new layer.

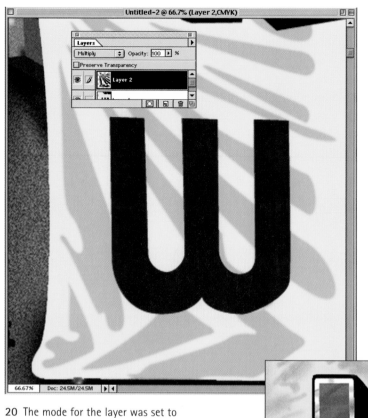

20 The mode for the layer was set to Multiply, and the opacity was lowered.

21 The Burn tool was used to add smaller folds and additional detail to the sign.

The opacity for the layer was lowered and the mode was changed to Multiply. Lowering the opacity allowed the sign in the layer beneath to show through (Figure 20). Changing the mode to Multiply makes the black increase the density of the yellow beneath, rather than just adding black to it.

To add more folds and details to the sign, I used the Burn tool and the Airbrush tool, with varying brush sizes (Figure 21).

Finally, I used the Add Noise filter (Filter>Noise>Add Noise) to add the texture and grit needed to complete the sign.

Phone Home

In Photoshop, the size of the phones would be too small to get any detail that would be satisfactory for me. Working larger in Illustrator and reducing in size for export to Photoshop was by far the superior method.

When I start a painting, I set up a formula that I will follow for creating elements in Illustrator. The size is determined by the amount of detail that will be required. A typical ratio is four to one. I create elements in Illustrator at 400%. This is four times the size that an element will appear in the Photoshop document. When I am ready to export to Photoshop, I reduce the element to 25%.

Meanwhile, back at the electronics shop… painting the vast variety of telephones for sale in the shop was another feat for Illustrator (Figure 22). Another great benefit of using Illustrator is that I didn't have to create so many different phones from scratch. I could make a few basic shapes and then modify them for variety.

22 The many phones on display at the shop were a task that required the versatility of Illustrator.

Using the tools in Illustrator, I created the basic phone, shown in Figure 23.

By duplicating that basic phone and making a few modifications, I started getting variety with little effort (Figure 24).

In all, the many phones visible in Figure 9 were created from some six or eight basic shapes. As with the sign, these phones were imported into Photoshop as pixels. In Photoshop, the highlights and shadows were added, using the tools available there.

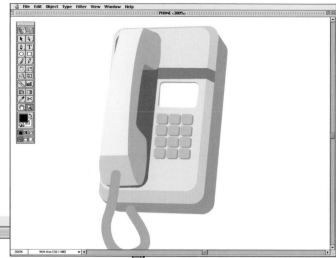

23 A basic phone shape was created in Illustrator.

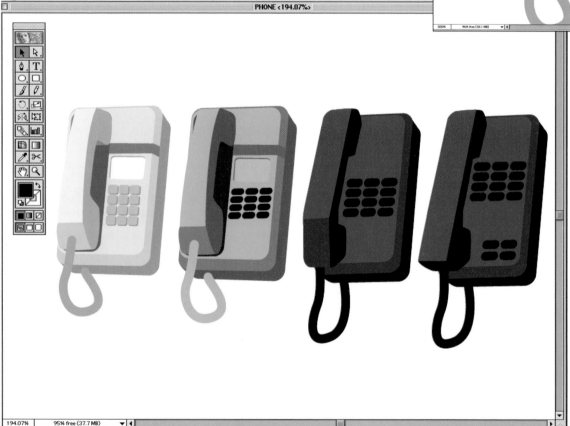

24 Many phones were made from that one basic shape.

25 The tire spokes on the bike are thinner than could have been created in Photoshop.

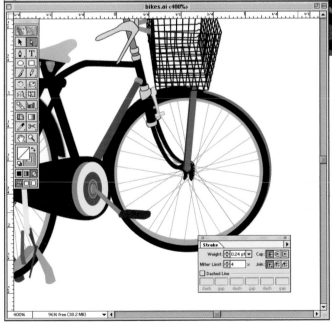

26 The tire spokes were created in Illustrator, using a .24 point stroke, and then brought into Photoshop.

Bicycle Spokes

The spokes on the bicycle tires are very thin (Figure 25). The Line tool in Photoshop is limited to a single pixel in width, which might be thin enough in most cases but was too thick for this painting. Take into account the anti-aliasing to make the line look smooth, and it gets thicker still.

Remember how Photoshop rasterizes the incoming Illustrator file? In Illustrator, I created the spokes and stroked them with a mere .24 point stroke (Figure 26). When I brought this very thin line into Photoshop, the result was an extremely fine line—much finer than I could have achieved with the Photoshop Line tool.

17

Realistic Newsprint

This rasterization process has come in handy on numerous occasions. Inside the newspaper bins in the *Pic-n-Pac* painting, newsprint is visible. To get that effect would be a trial-and-error process, not to mention time consuming. By creating actual text in Illustrator (Figure 27) and rasterizing it into Photoshop (Figure 28), I simplified the process.

To create the title of the newspaper on the side of the bin I used the same technique used in the Japanese signage in *Akihabara* (Figure 29).

27 The text of the newspaper in the Illustrator file.

28 The text of the newspaper in the Photoshop file.

29 The title of the newspaper on the side of the bin was done in the same manner as the text on the Japanese signs.

Flyers on a Pole

The flyers pasted on the pole announced a concert, and I wanted them to be accurate. I duplicated the information on the flyer in an Illustrator file (Figure 30), imported the file into Photoshop, and then cropped it to simulate the flyer wrapped around the pole (Figure 31).

The majority of the elements were created in this manner, using Illustrator.

30 The text of the concert flyer in the Illustrator file.

31 The text of the concert flyer on the pole in the Photoshop file.

19

Details, Details...

Figure 32 shows a detail of *Pic-n-Pac*, the inside of the store visible through the door and window. Figure 33 shows the elements in their Illustrator format. Notice that the original Illustrator images are flat and lack shading. All the shading and highlights were added in the Photoshop document.

Occasionally I use the Illustrator/Photoshop combination to add a little fun to the image. I did an image called *Future City* back in 1992, using Photoshop 2.0. Photoshop didn't have layers then, but the Illustrator/Photoshop connection was there.

The close-up of a window in the painting shows a man at work at his desk (Figure 34). The CDs on his desk, reproduced in Figure 35, have titles on them. Figure 36 shows the entire image.

32 This detailed close-up from the Photoshop file shows the inside of the store through the window and door.

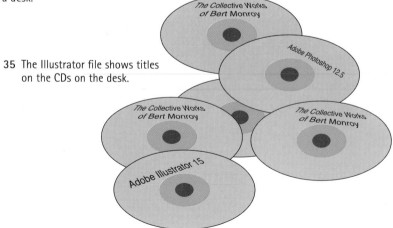

33 The elements used for the detail of Figure 32 are shown here in the Illustrator file.

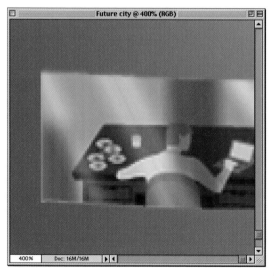

34 The window on the lower right of the image shows a man sitting at a desk.

35 The Illustrator file shows titles on the CDs on the desk.

36 The image *Future City* was created with Photoshop 2.0 in 1992.

Using the Illustrator Pattern Brush

Illustrator has other features that make it the ideal software for creating the elements for an image. For one, Illustrator now has a Pattern Brush, which works differently than what one might associate with a typical pattern. When you think of patterns, wallpaper usually comes to mind. (Chapter 8, "Creating Textures from Patterns," is dedicated to the typical creation and use of textures from patterns.) The Pattern Brush uses a contiguous shape to stroke a line.

Figure 37 shows a detail from *Rendez-vous*, a painting that is also used in Chapter 4, "Shading." Note the chain that connects the sign to its bracket.

Normally, I would be inclined to paint each of those links. Or perhaps I would create one link, duplicate it many times, and rotate each duplicate into position on the chain. That is the way I used to tackle this sort of problem. Version 8 of Illustrator changed all that. Read on to discover how I made this chain.

In Illustrator, I created the basic link by making an elliptical shape (Figure 38). Then I created a second, smaller ellipse and centered it inside the first (Figure 39).

37 This detail is taken from the painting *Rendez-vous*. Notice the chain on the side of the sidewalk sign. It was created with the new Pattern Brush in Illustrator.

38 In Illustrator, an ellipse was created.

39 A second ellipse was created inside and centered within the first.

With the Scissors tool, I cut the ellipses at each point on the top and bottom, and also on both sides. This created four separate curved lines for each ellipse. I then used the Join command to join the end points of each curve of the large ellipse to the corresponding end points of the same curve of the small ellipse. This made four distinct sections of a single chain link, which I filled with a brown color. Figure 40 shows the four sections. They appear to be separated from each other, but this was done purely for the purpose of showing the distinction. The pieces were not separated.

The two shapes on the left were cloned, moved over to the right to form an interlocking effect with the original link, and then filled with a light brown color (Figure 41).

Then, with the Reflect tool, I cloned the two light-brown curved sections on a vertical axis (Figure 42). I used the center of the original link as the point for the Reflect axis.

The two top sections of the original link were brought to the front. This completed the look of an interlocking chain link (Figure 43).

40 The two ellipses were cut and joined together to form four distinct shapes.

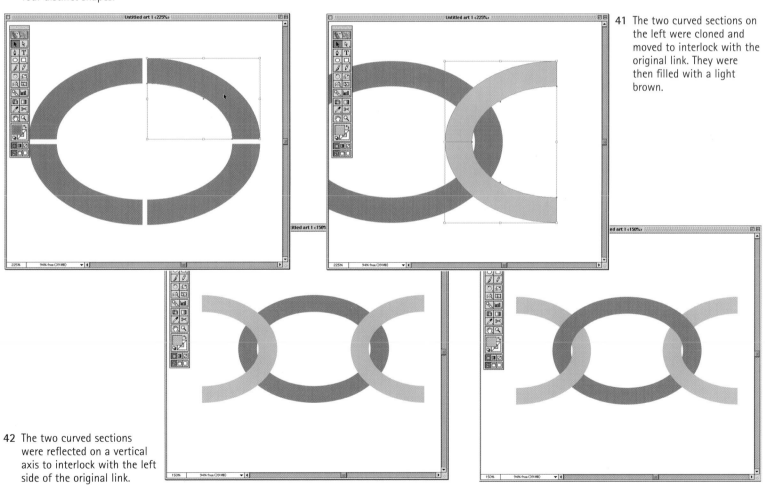

41 The two curved sections on the left were cloned and moved to interlock with the original link. They were then filled with a light brown.

42 The two curved sections were reflected on a vertical axis to interlock with the left side of the original link.

43 The two curved sections on the top of the original link were brought to the front to complete the look of a chain link.

Just for the sake of cleanliness, I used the Pathfinder option to join the sections for the top of the original link into a single section (Figure 44). Then I did the same to the link's two lower sections (Figure 45).

The sections that made up the side links had to remain as separate sections; their positions had to remain intact to create the effect of a chain link. One appeared in front of the center link while the other was placed in back.

Next I had to create the path for the chain that would eventually be made of the link I had just created in Illustrator. Switching to Photoshop, I used the Path tool to create a path for the chain (Figure 46) and copied this path to the Clipboard.

In Illustrator, the path for the chain was pasted into the document where the link had been created (Figure 47).

44 The two curved sections were joined to form a single section.

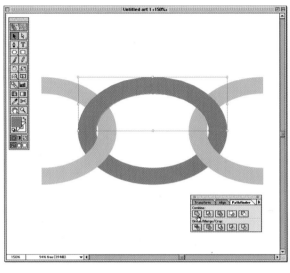

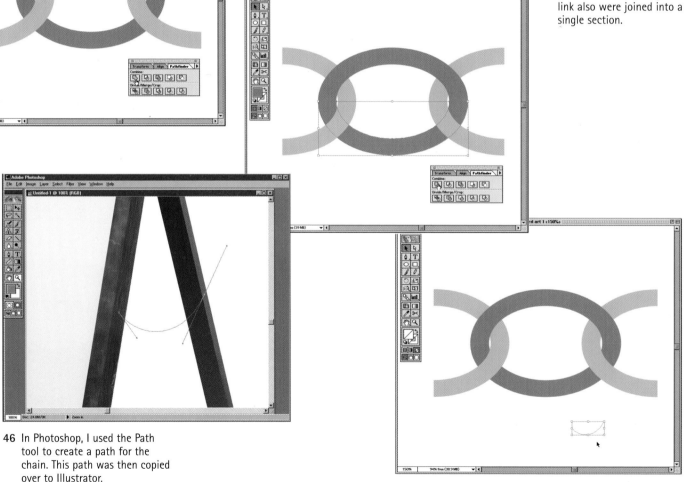

45 The two curved sections on the bottom of the original link also were joined into a single section.

46 In Photoshop, I used the Path tool to create a path for the chain. This path was then copied over to Illustrator.

47 The path for the chain was pasted into the Illustrator file with the link.

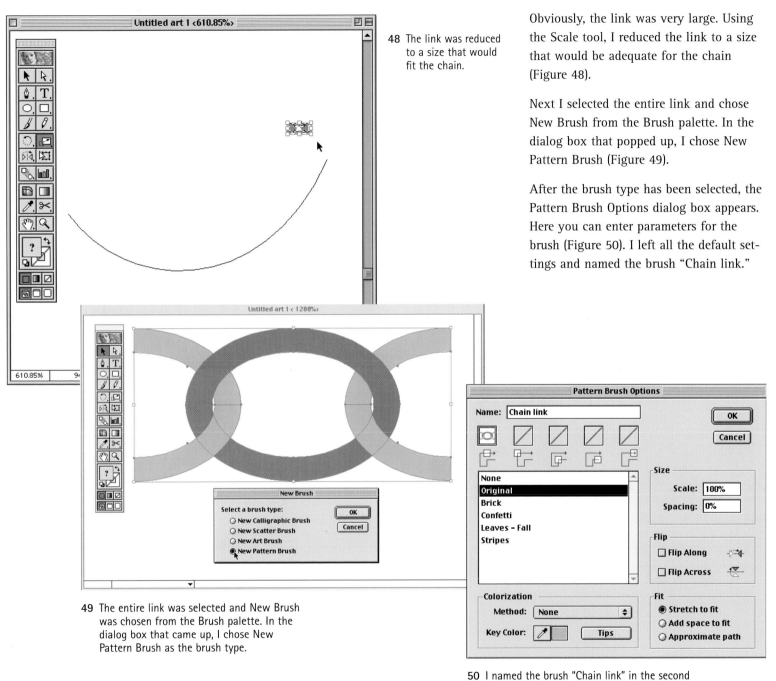

48 The link was reduced to a size that would fit the chain.

49 The entire link was selected and New Brush was chosen from the Brush palette. In the dialog box that came up, I chose New Pattern Brush as the brush type.

50 I named the brush "Chain link" in the second dialog box that is associated with the creation of a new brush. The default settings were left as-is.

Obviously, the link was very large. Using the Scale tool, I reduced the link to a size that would be adequate for the chain (Figure 48).

Next I selected the entire link and chose New Brush from the Brush palette. In the dialog box that popped up, I chose New Pattern Brush (Figure 49).

After the brush type has been selected, the Pattern Brush Options dialog box appears. Here you can enter parameters for the brush (Figure 50). I left all the default settings and named the brush "Chain link."

The newly created pattern brush then appeared in the Brushes palette. I selected the path for the chain and clicked on the pattern brush in the palette. The path was transformed into a chain (Figure 51).

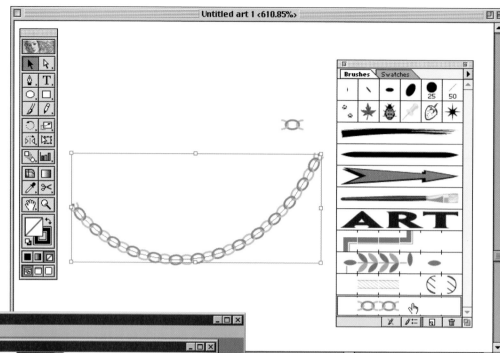

51 The path was stroked with the pattern of the chain link.

This completed chain was copied to the Clipboard and imported to Photoshop for inclusion into the painting (Figure 52).

For another example of these unique brushes, see Chapter 6, "Creating a Greener World."

52 The path with the chain link was copied to the clipboard and copied over to Photoshop.

Following the Paths to *the gate*

Earlier in this chapter, I mentioned that paths created in Illustrator can be imported into Photoshop as pixels or paths. I have demonstrated importing paths as pixels. Now I'll show you how and why to import as paths.

The image *the gate* was created on location using a PowerBook (Figure 53). I spent five days sitting at the site, creating all the paths for the image in Illustrator. Four evenings were spent turning those paths into selections in Photoshop, to be filled with the appropriate colors.

The first thing I did was determine the overall dimensions for the final image. I decided it would measure 12 by 9 1/2 inches; then, in Illustrator, I created a box with those dimensions.

53 I used a PowerBook and created the image *the gate* on location.

The Basic Shapes

The paths for the basic shapes were all
created in Illustrator (Figure 54). They were
all included in a single file so that the proper proportions and positions would match
the scene.

When all the paths had been completed,
I was ready to export them to Photoshop.
I rely on the copy-and-paste method.
Photoshop does have the capability to
export your paths to Illustrator. From
Illustrator, you can do the drag-and-drop
routine: In Illustrator, select the object or
objects. Then with the Command key (Ctrl
on the PC) held down, drag the selection
over onto a Photoshop document.

Copy and paste is still my preferred method.
I don't have to be concerned with windows
being visible. Most important, paths are tiny
bits of information that, unlike pixel data,
does not take up a massive amount of
RAM when copied to the Clipboard. The
back-and-forth process is fast.

When I pasted the paths into Photoshop, I chose the Paste As
Paths option (Figure 55). The paths fell into the Paths palette as a
Work Path (Figure 56). I immediately saved the path.

> **n o t e** | A Work Path is temporary and can be easily lost. If the
> Work Path is not selected, use of the Path tool will automatically
> replace the contents of the Work Path as soon as you make a
> single click.

Each path represented a specific element in the overall image. I
proceeded to separate the paths into individual paths for use in
the painting.

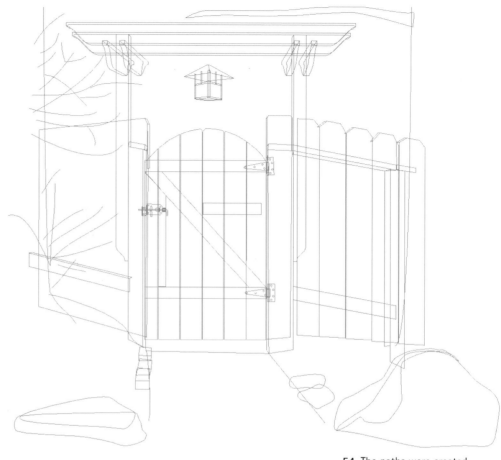

54 The paths were created
in a single Illustrator file.

55 The paths from the Illustrator
file were imported into
Photoshop as paths.

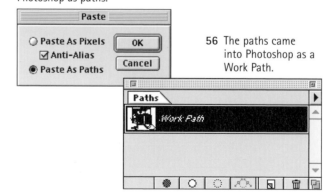

56 The paths came
into Photoshop as a
Work Path.

The Hinges

The hardware for the gate, for example, was placed in its own path. That path was further separated to enable me to create the bolts that attached the hinges to the gate (Figure 57).

A new layer was created to contain the various parts of the hardware. Each path was then turned into a selection and filled with the appropriate color (Figure 58).

The flat color was subjected to sprays of darker colors with the Airbrush tool to simulate the stains of weathering on the metal (Figure 59).

The Add Noise filter (Filter>Noise>Add Noise) was applied to add a texture to the hinge (Figure 60). I entered a small number for the amount of noise because I just wanted a soft texture to simulate aging and wear. Too much noise would have made the hinge look as though it had a rough texture, like sandpaper.

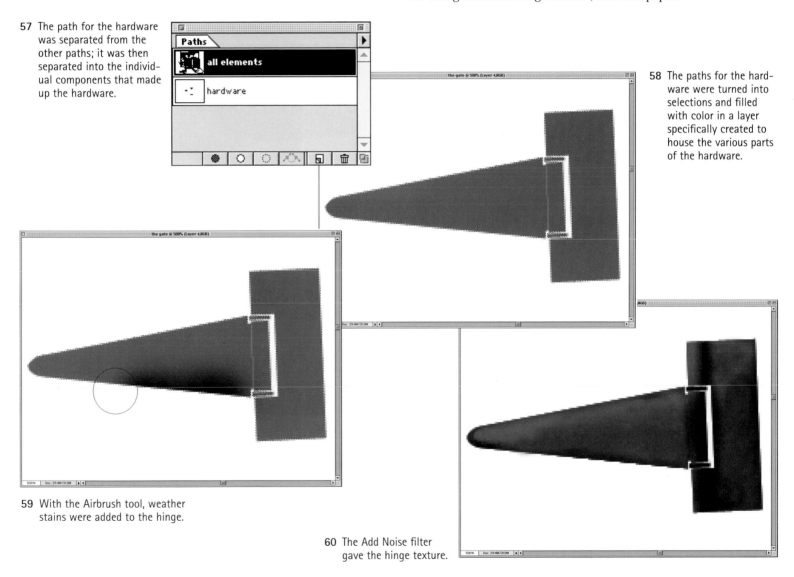

57 The path for the hardware was separated from the other paths; it was then separated into the individual components that made up the hardware.

58 The paths for the hardware were turned into selections and filled with color in a layer specifically created to house the various parts of the hardware.

59 With the Airbrush tool, weather stains were added to the hinge.

60 The Add Noise filter gave the hinge texture.

Next came the bolts that attach the hinge to the gate. I created a layer for the bolts, turned their paths into selections, and filled them with a radial gradient made from gray to a darker gray (Figure 61).

In a layer created behind the layer of the bolts (Figure 62), I created their shadow. The shadow was a mixture of actual shadow and the corrosion residue that occurs in a metal hinge of this type. I used the Airbrush tool, with black for the color, and a brush size to match the area of the shadow and corrosion stain. A simple click in the layer was all that was necessary.

When all the elements of the hinge were completed, the various layers that made up the hinge were merged into a single layer, which was then duplicated. Preserve Transparency was turned on for the duplicate layer, and it was filled with black.

Then Preserve Transparency was turned off, and a Gaussian Blur filter (Filter>Blur>Gaussian Blur) was applied. A small amount of blur was used—just enough to soften the edges. That layer was then moved behind the layer of the hinge, to act as a shadow. With the Move tool and the cursor keys, the shadow layer was lowered to sit below the hinge (Figure 63).

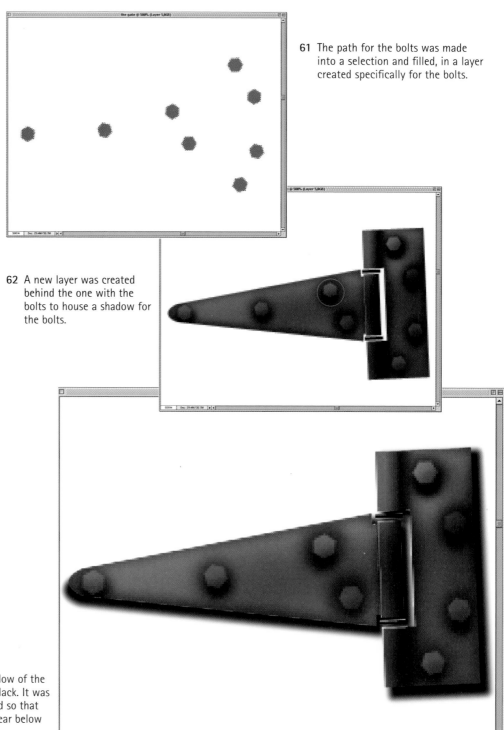

61 The path for the bolts was made into a selection and filled, in a layer created specifically for the bolts.

62 A new layer was created behind the one with the bolts to house a shadow for the bolts.

63 The layer with the shadow of the hinge was filled with black. It was then blurred and moved so that the shadow would appear below the hinge.

The Spring

Certain parts of the painting were created entirely in Illustrator, with simple shading added in Photoshop (Figure 64). In certain instances, the tools in Illustrator do things to paths that can't be done in Photoshop. The spring visible on the side of the gate was one of these instances.

The spring started out as a small circle, filled with a beige color, in Illustrator (Figure 65). With the Reflect tool, I duplicated the circle on a vertical axis (Figure 66). Then I created a rectangle that connected the two circles (Figure 67). All three objects were turned into a single object with the Unite/Pathfinder function (Figure 68).

64 The spring on the gate was created in Illustrator.

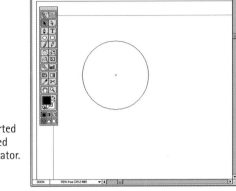

65 The spring started as a beige-filled circle in Illustrator.

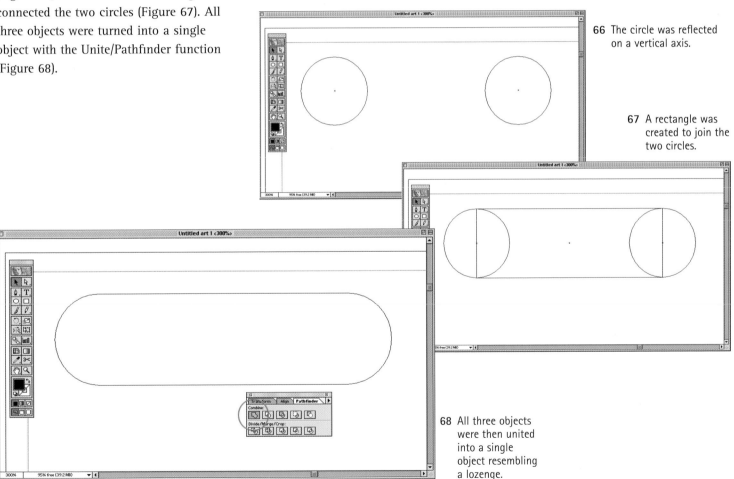

66 The circle was reflected on a vertical axis.

67 A rectangle was created to join the two circles.

68 All three objects were then united into a single object resembling a lozenge.

With the Rotate tool, I angled the direction of the lozenge. I cloned the lozenge directly below the original. By pressing Command+D (Ctrl+D on the PC), which is Transform Again, the clone was duplicated again and again, until I had created the entire length of the spring (Figure 69).

I selected all the objects and then, using the Reflect tool, I made a copy that was flipped on a vertical axis.

This new set was filled with a dark gray color and sent to the back of the original spring sections. This new set served as the back part of the spring, visible through the coils in front (Figure 70).

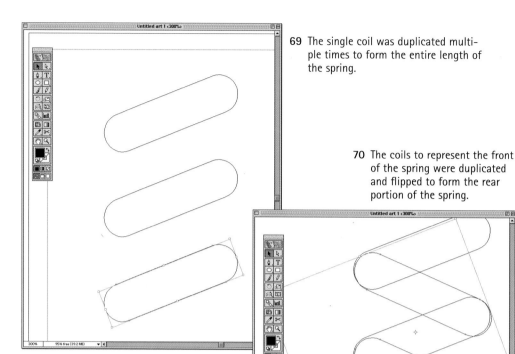

69 The single coil was duplicated multiple times to form the entire length of the spring.

70 The coils to represent the front of the spring were duplicated and flipped to form the rear portion of the spring.

71 The additional hardware of the spring was added to the top and bottom.

I drew the additional hardware at the top and bottom of the coils (Figure 71). Then I filled various objects with colors that represent both the metal and the colors created by the different angles reflecting the light off the metal.

72 The spring was imported into Photoshop and rotated into position.

The finished spring was imported into Photoshop (Figure 72). There, it was rotated to the angle needed for placement within the scene. The Dodge and Burn tools were used to add shadows and highlights to the spring (Figure 73). Other aspects of this painting will be discussed later in other chapters.

So now you have seen the approach I take to the creation of a painting. So many additional considerations come into play. In the next chapter, I show you the details of what goes into the preparation of a scene—what holds it together and draws the viewer into it.

73 The Dodge and Burn tools were used to add shadows and highlights.

chapter 2

Perspective

If you take a look at my paintings in the gallery and throughout the book, one thing you will notice is that I never paint a subject straight on. I always portray my subjects at an angle. The angle can be very intense, as in *The Studio theater* (Figure 1). Or the angle might be slight, as in the painting *Peter's Ice Cream* (Figure 2). I like to play with angles because I feel they add dimension to a scene. Angles also carry the viewer's eye to some imaginary place beyond the boundary of the painting, placing the scene into context with its surroundings, even though the rest of the scene is not visible.

1 The perspective in *The Studio theater* is much more pronounced.

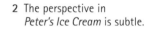

2 The perspective in *Peter's Ice Cream* is subtle.

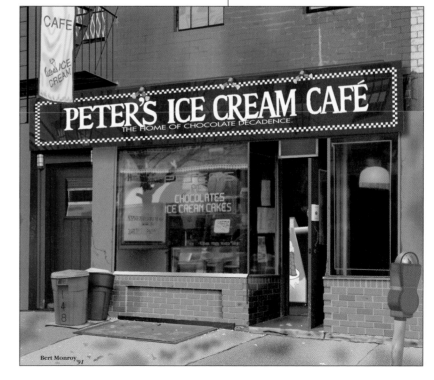

Bert Monroy '91

Even my commercial paintings tend to have angles—provided the client approves. The two commercial examples, (SitComm and CDW), Figures 3 and 4, demonstrate how I took the client's basic idea and improved on it. In both cases, the client's original sketch had a flat, head-on shot of the product. In order to add life and movement to the image, I introduced perspective.

Adding the effect of a third dimension gives the viewer a sense of movement within the image. It also adds an element of excitement to an otherwise simple image. Perspective allows us to portray, in a two-dimensional format, the complex, three-dimensional world we inhabit and make it believable. It is like taking a portion of our perceived reality and putting a scale model of it in a display case for others to see.

When I first approach a subject to paint, I will deliberately study it from exaggerated angles. These angles can serve many purposes, depending on what I am trying to emphasize.

Exaggerated perspective can also be used to create dramatic effects in an illustration. Getting a worm's eye view, for example, can be achieved by using a strong perspective—one that has the vanishing point at the apex of the observer's point of view.

3 The SitComm project.

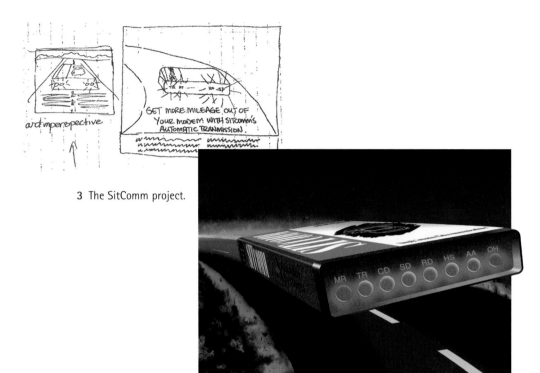

4 The CDW project.

Fundamental Terms

To understand the process of creating images with proper perspective, it is crucial to understand certain fundamental terms:

- Horizon
- Vertical measuring line
- Horizon line
- Ground line
- Vanishing points
- Vanishing lines

These terms are defined and described in the following sections.

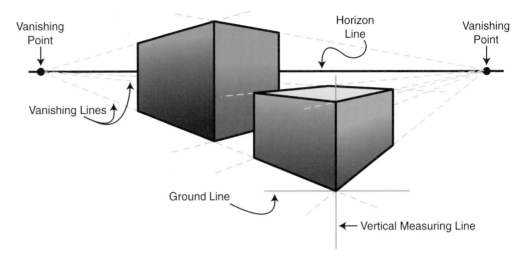

5 Study the different aspects of perspective.

Horizon

All the elements within an image are created from the point of view of the person looking at the image. The *horizon* is the eye level of the person viewing the scene. When you place the horizon below the ground line, you create the view you would get if you were an insect. When you place the horizon line near the ground line, you create a normal view. When you place the horizon above the objects in a scene, you create the view you would get if you were flying above the scene.

Horizon Line

The *horizon line* is basically the plane at which the land and sky meet, off in the distance. The horizon line is always a straight line, even though the Earth is round. Establishing this horizon line is crucial, even if buildings, hills, or other elements in the image obscure it.

Vertical Measuring Line

The *vertical measuring line* is an imaginary line drawn from the bottom to the top of the object closest to the person viewing the scene. This vertical measuring line determines two aspects of a scene: the height of objects in the scene and what you see in the scene. Placing the vertical measuring line on the left allows you to see more of the right side of the object. Placing the line on the right allows you to see more of the left side of the object.

Ground Line

The *ground line,* also referred to as the *ground plane,* is the bottom of the object being rendered or the place where it touches the ground.

Vanishing Points

Vanishing points are the points on the horizon where parallel horizontal lines converge.

Vanishing Lines

Vanishing lines are the horizontal lines of the object, which converge on the vanishing points.

How do we determine how perspective works? Figure 5 demonstrates exactly how perspective works. All the different aspects of perspective are outlined. Notice that the relationship between the two boxes and their environment is effective in creating the illusion of spatial reality.

One-Point Perspective

As we view the world, all objects that fall into our field of vision follow invisible lines that converge on the horizon line. If you were to stand in the middle of a city street facing the direction the street is receding, you could draw imaginary lines along the edges of the sidewalk to a point off in the distance where the sky meets the street. If you then drew more lines that follow the tops of the buildings and all the tops and bottoms of the windows, you would find that all the lines converge at the same point (Figure 6). That point is known as the vanishing point, and your view is considered a *one-point perspective*.

As objects get farther away from the viewer, they diminish in size along what are known as vanishing lines. Likewise, the edges of the side of an object visible to the viewer diminish in visual size as those edges get farther from the viewer. All the angles follow the vanishing lines and converge on the horizon at the vanishing point.

Two-Point Perspective

When more than one side of an object or structure is visible, it is necessary to create multiple vanishing points that all converge on the same horizon line. If you were back on that street corner and started looking at the corner on the opposite side of the street, you would now have the view of two streets receding into the distance (Figure 7). This is a *two-point perspective*. Both points still converge on a single horizon line.

6 When you use one-point perspective in portraying the view down a city street, all the vanishing lines converge at the vanishing point.

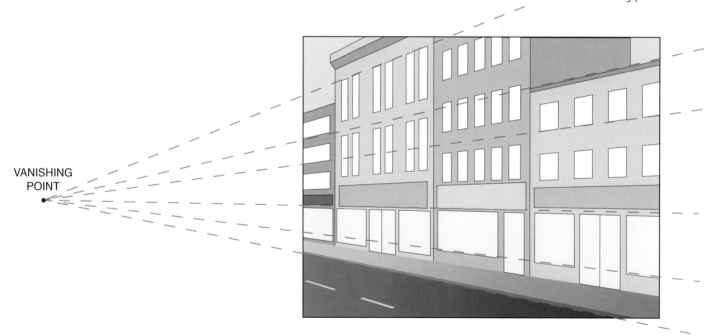

VANISHING
POINT

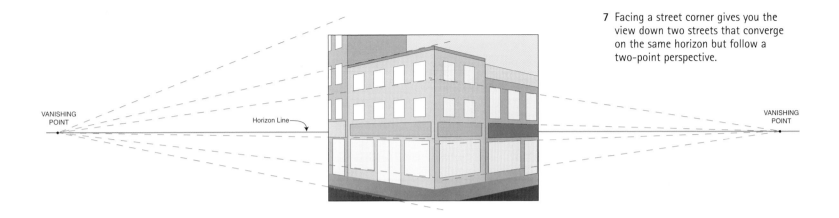

7 Facing a street corner gives you the view down two streets that converge on the same horizon but follow a two-point perspective.

VANISHING POINT

Horizon Line

VANISHING POINT

8 Because the back of the box is the same size as the front, this box has no perspective.

9 Because this box has two-point perspective, it looks three-dimensional.

Putting Things into Perspective

The box in Figure 8 has no perspective. The back of the box is the same size as the front. It seems as though the back is slightly larger than the front. Something is not right with this picture.

The box in Figure 9, on the other hand, has a two-point perspective added to its edges. You will notice that it seems to be three-dimensional, or at least a bit more realistic than the box in Figure 8. Perspective made all the difference.

Figure 10 shows the same box viewed from three different types of perspective. Notice the drastic change from one shape to the next.

10 These boxes are basically the same shape, but each is viewed from a different perspective.

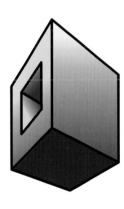

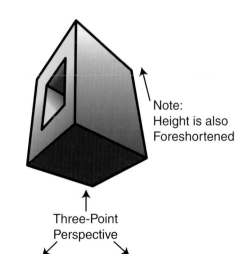

Note: Height is also Foreshortened

One-Point Perspective

Two-Point Perspective

Three-Point Perspective

11 The vanishing point for this scene is way off to the right.

12 The vanishing point for this scene is dead center, as if you were standing in the middle of the road.

By studying the photographs in Figures 11, 12, and 13, you can see how these fundamentals work in reality.

Neither Illustrator nor Photoshop has the capability to render three-dimensional objects. They are 2D drawing and imaging programs. However, many 3D programs are available. If 3D is necessary and you have the time to create and render such an image, using a 3D package will solve many of your problems.

13 This scene also has the vanishing point in the center. Notice that every line in the image converges on that point.

Getting a Perspective on Things

In Illustrator and Photoshop, it is sometimes necessary to simulate a third dimension in two-dimensional space. To do this, I start out by deciding on the angle I am trying to achieve. In Illustrator, I set up a file with a box that has the dimensions of what the final image will be. Within this box, I draw basic lines that outline the vertical position of the subject of the overall scene (Figure 14). These lines serve as guides when the objects are rendered. I then establish the position of the horizon line and draw a line to represent it in the scene.

To this horizon line, I draw the vanishing lines for the elements in the image, to serve as guides, meeting at the vanishing points (Figure 15).

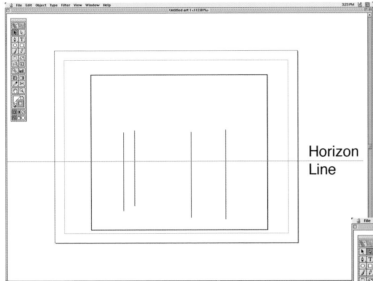

Horizon
Line

14 Within the box that has the outer dimensions of the image, the horizon line is established and guides are created to outline the vertical position of the subject of the image.

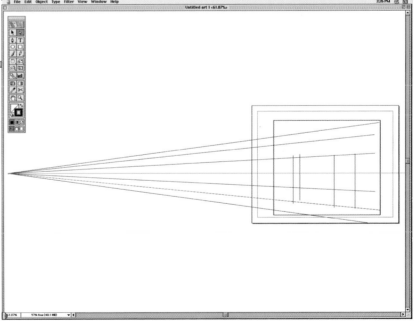

15 To the horizon line, guides are generated for all the vanishing lines.

I convert these lines into actual guides (View>Make Guides) as seen in Figure 16. I make sure that the guides are not locked so that I can move them into different positions as I need them. I also make duplicate sets for additional sides of an object that need to follow the same perspective (Figure 17). If I am illustrating a building, these additional guides could be used for the windows or other architectural details.

If two-point perspective is necessary, all the guides created can be easily flipped horizontally to create the guides to the other vanishing point, to avoid having to create new ones.

Using the Direct Selection tool, you can select individual points of the guides and then reposition them wherever they're needed (Figure 18). The point situated at the vanishing point on the horizon line never moves, however, because it ensures accurate placement of vanishing lines for all the objects in an image.

Even when I create the elements of an image entirely in Photoshop, I still create the initial guides in Illustrator. Here's why: In Photoshop, the dimensions of the image are the dimensions of the file. In Illustrator, the drawing area far exceeds the dimensions of the image, giving you the ability to have a much larger work area than the one Photoshop gives you.

You could create in Photoshop a file large enough to accommodate the additional area and then just crop the vanishing points later. However, you really don't want to do that. If your image is 300dpi and 10 inches by 12 inches, for example, you need an additional 20 inches on the sides to establish the vanishing points. Whew! We're talking a serious file size. RAM? Forget about it!

16 Lines that are generated in Illustrator can be converted into guides.

17 These guides are unlocked so that they can be moved into various positions as necessary.

18 With the Direct Selection tool, the end points of the guides can be moved as necessary.

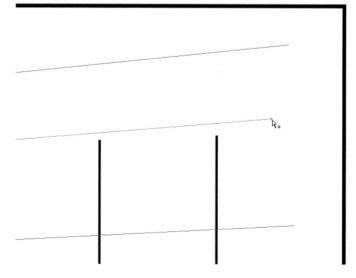

Exercise 2.1 Stepping through Imported Guides

When your final image is a Photoshop document, I recommend that you follow these steps to establish the perspective:

1 In Illustrator, generate a box the dimensions of the final image that will be in Photoshop.

2 Draw the horizon line.

3 Establish the vanishing points.

4 Draw a single line to represent the top of the basic object or structure in the image (Figure 19).

5 Draw another line to represent the bottom of the object or structure (Figure 20).

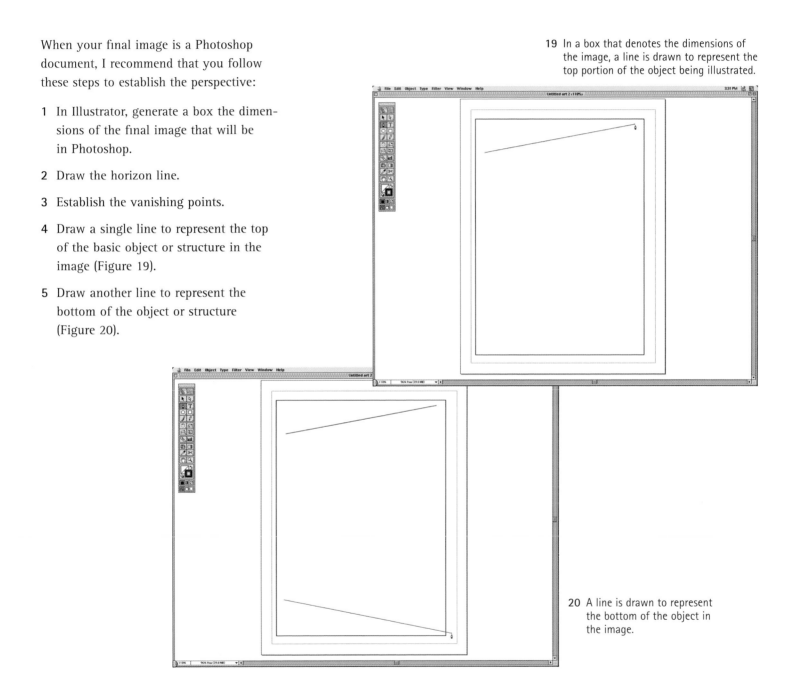

19 In a box that denotes the dimensions of the image, a line is drawn to represent the top portion of the object being illustrated.

20 A line is drawn to represent the bottom of the object in the image.

Exercise 2.1   Stepping through Imported Guides *(continued)*

6 Using the Blend tool, create a blend from the top line to the bottom line.

I choose as many steps as I feel I will need to give me enough lines to use as guides (Figure 21). For example, if the structure to be illustrated is a skyscraper with many windows, I create many lines. A structure with fewer horizontal details needs fewer steps for the blend.

7 Import all the lines into Photoshop, placing them into a layer that serves as a guide for creating the elements of the image (Figure 22).

8 If you have additional vanishing points for other views, place those guides into separate layers to make it easy to distinguish one from the other, thus eliminating any possible confusion.

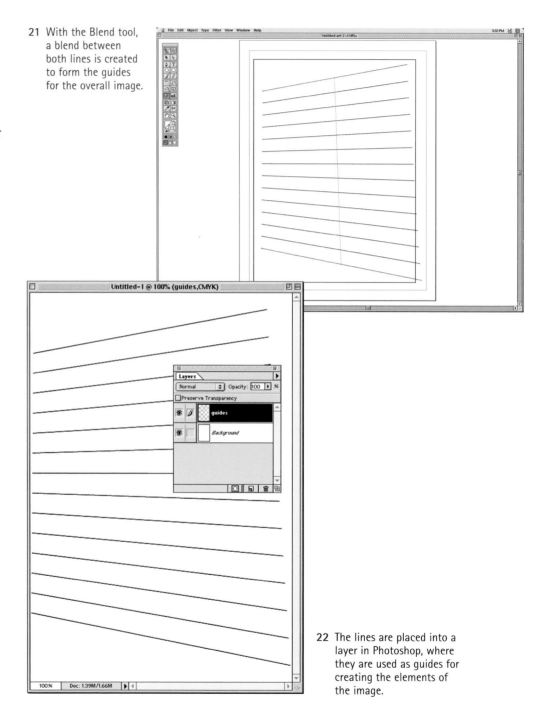

21 With the Blend tool, a blend between both lines is created to form the guides for the overall image.

22 The lines are placed into a layer in Photoshop, where they are used as guides for creating the elements of the image.

23 The three-point perspective in this figure gives you a feeling of being very small and looking up at an immense object.

An Exaggerated Perspective

Exaggerated perspective can be effective in creating certain moods. One of the most frequent uses for exaggerated perspective is to create the illusion of immensity. It is also used to offer a different point of view. Rather than base the perspective of the scene on the view of a person standing on the ground, you might want to use the view a person would have if she were looking down from a plane. Or perhaps you might want to use the view an ant would have when it looks up at our world.

You create these exaggerated views when you use three-point perspective. Three-point perspective comes into play when you look up or down at an object. If you take a photograph looking up at a building, you will notice that the sides of the building lean in toward the center of the picture. This happens because they are as subject to the laws of perspective as any other plane receding from our view. Adding a third vanishing point in the vertical plane takes into account the convergence of the vertical lines of an object. While it does not have to result in an exaggerated perspective, three-point perspective can be used to create the effect of immensity.

Figure 23 shows the effect of an exaggerated three-point perspective to denote immensity. The viewer might be an employee on the way to ask for a raise.

Figure 24 gives you a view from a plane, looking down at a city. This is an old MacPaint image I created back in 1985 for a comic book.

24 In this 1985 MacPaint image, three-point perspective was used to give you an exaggerated bird's-eye view.

In the two images that were commissioned by an ad agency for Apple Computer, I used three-point perspective to accentuate the structure and give movement to the compositions (Figures 25 and 26).

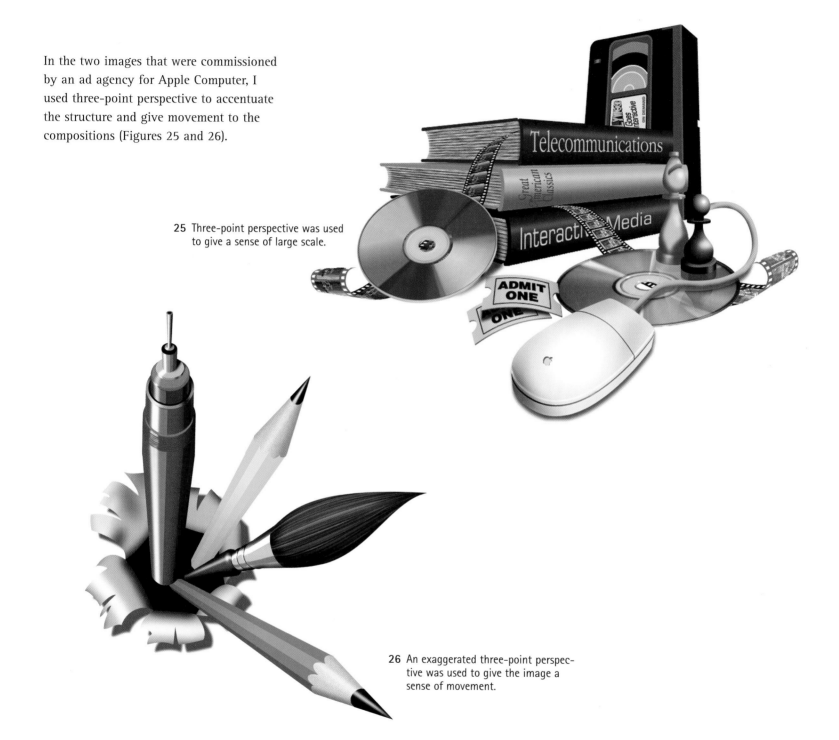

25 Three-point perspective was used to give a sense of large scale.

26 An exaggerated three-point perspective was used to give the image a sense of movement.

Atmospheric Perspective

There is another aspect of perspective that I usually do not consider in my paintings—atmospheric perspective. This is basically an interference with visual perception that causes a loss of detail, contrast, and focus as objects get farther from the viewer. In my paintings, I want the viewer to be there. Any place within the image will be in focus.

This loss of detail, contrast, and focus is most evident in the focal plane of a camera. Look at any photograph you have taken of people in front of a vast vista in the background. If you focused on the people in the foreground, the background will be out of focus.

Your eyes work in much the same way. Look at an object close to you and you will notice that all else is blurred. Look in the distance and objects up close are blurred.

If you want to get this effect for your images, all you have to do is blur the elements that are not the focal point of the illustration, as in Figure 27. The objects off in the distance were subjected to the Gaussian Blur filter.

27 By blurring elements that are not the focal point of an illustration, you draw attention to the object being highlighted and create a true photographic look.

Matching Perspective

As we have seen, perspective plays an important role in the creation of an image. When you are compositing multiple images, it is crucial to match the attributes of all the images being brought in to the attributes of the original image or background. Various considerations, such as the lighting and shadows caused by the light source, must be taken into account. Of equal importance is perspective.

Proper perspective will make the composite believable. If the perspective does not match, even an untrained eye will find the disparity in the composite.

In order to match the perspective of the original image, it is necessary to create a series of grids for the perspective. You can then use these grids as guides for the distortion of the composited element so that the perspective of the element matches the perspective of the background into which it is being composited.

The image in Figure 28 has very strong angles. To place an additional image onto the steps in the scene, you must give that image the same angles as the steps.

The first thing to do is to establish the vanishing points on the horizon. By visually following the straight edges of the building and steps, you can see that they converge outside the boundary of the image.

28 This image has very strong angles. Any image being brought into this one has to match these angles to appear to be part of the scene.

Exercise 2.2 Stepping through Cropping Guides

To set up your vanishing points, it is
necessary, in this exercise, to extend the
boundaries of the image. To achieve this,
the canvas must be enlarged. Since the
current dimensions of the image are to be
the final dimensions, you must create a
guide to make it easy to crop later. Follow
these steps:

1 To make the cropping guide, choose
   Select>Select All.

2 Choose Save Selection to turn the
   selected area into an alpha channel.
   This alpha channel will make it easy to
   make the proper crop later.

3 Choose Image>Canvas Size to enlarge
   the work area.

   Additional space is given to the width
   of the image—enough space to encompass the point at which all vanishing
   lines converge (Figure 29). The new
   canvas should have plenty of room on
   either side of the original image
   (Figure 30). Note that the original
   image is kept centered.

4 Create a new layer to contain the grid.

5 Select the Line tool, using a contrasting color and a width thick enough for
   the line to be seen over the image.

6 Draw a line following one of the
   straight edges at the bottom of the
   image to a point well outside the area
   of the image (Figure 31).

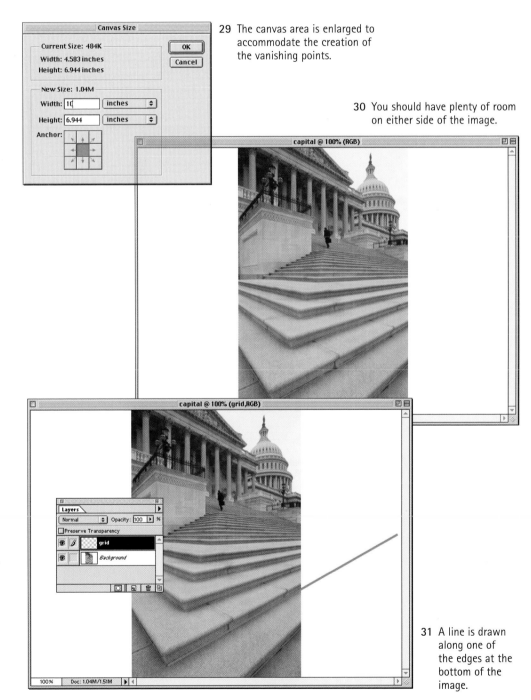

29 The canvas area is enlarged to
   accommodate the creation of
   the vanishing points.

30 You should have plenty of room
   on either side of the image.

31 A line is drawn
   along one of
   the edges at the
   bottom of the
   image.

49

Exercise 2.2   Stepping through Cropping Guides *(continued)*

7   Draw a second line following one of the edges at the top. The point at which the two converge is the vanishing point (Figure 32).

8   Follow the same procedure for the opposite side of the elements in the image (Figure 33).

n o t e | If you were to draw a line from one vanishing point to the other, this straight horizontal line would be the horizon line.

9   In a new layer and with a different color, draw the vertical measuring line or the part of the object closest to the person viewing the object (Figure 34).

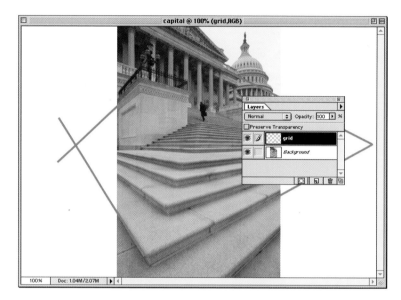

32 A second line is drawn along a top edge of the image. The two lines converge at the vanishing point.

33 Lines are drawn on the opposite side of the image to establish the vanishing point on the left.

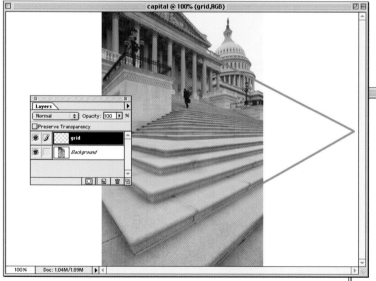

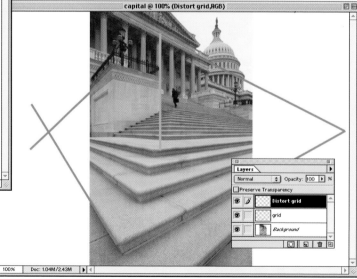

34 A line to signify the edge of the object closest to you is drawn.

50

10 Import the new object into the image, placing it so that the edge of the front cover is directly over the vertical measuring line (Figure 35).

11 Draw the guides for perspective from the top and bottom of the vertical line where you want the top and bottom of the new element to rest (Figure 36). These lines are drawn to converge on the vanishing points. Do this to both sides of the object's grid.

12 Select the front of the object to be distorted and use the Distort (Edit>Transform>Distort) feature to distort the front to match the grid.

13 Reduce the width of the object so as to create the foreshortening necessary to get believable results (Figure 37).

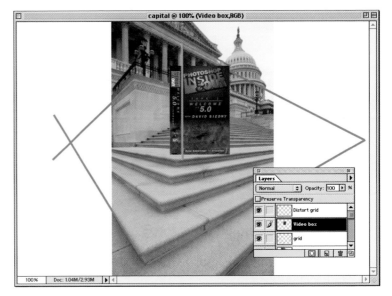

35 The object is imported into the image and placed in position so that the edge is directly over the vertical measuring line.

36 Lines are drawn from the top and bottom of the measuring line, at the points where the object rests, to converge on the vanishing point.

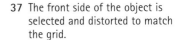

37 The front side of the object is selected and distorted to match the grid.

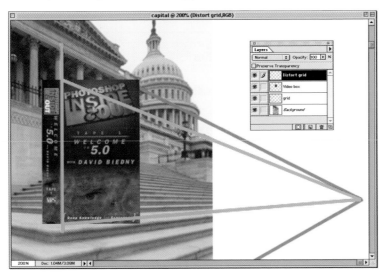

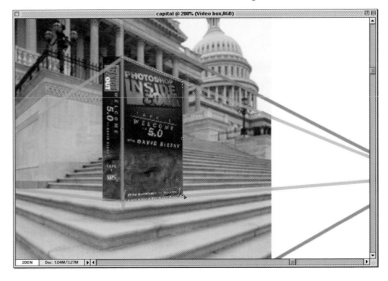

Exercise 2.2 Stepping through Cropping Guides *(continued)*

n o t e | To understand the concept of foreshortening, let's do a little experiment. Take this book and hold it up in front of you—with the cover facing you. Turn the book slightly to the side so that the left edge of the book is closer to you and the right edge is further away. Notice that the width of the book cover seems to get thinner. The vertical lines of the edges get closer together. This is an optical illusion. You know the book didn't really get thinner; it just looks that way. You do know that, right? Well, this optical illusion is what you have to recreate in the two-dimensional world of Photoshop.

14 Distort the other side of the object in the same fashion.

The result, shown in Figure 38, is matched perspective, which makes the composite look real.

38 The final composite is believable.

chapter 3

Lighting

As a photorealist painter, the switch to the computer was a natural progression. I paint what I see; therefore, painting with light is my preferred way of working.

I love the play of light on objects. Trying to re-create that play has always been my most enjoyable challenge. The summers in California have given me a new outlook on the play of lights and shadows. The California sun is very bright and clear. It tends to oversaturate the colors of a scene. California has a strong sense of color in its architecture, which is a natural response to its colorful landscapes.

Night Light

Artificial light can be striking, too. It can have competing light sources that illuminate a scene from different angles. Artificial lighting also has a direct relationship with the objects that come within its range. This can create a myriad of shadows–but that's another chapter (the next one). Artificial light also comes in colors.

In this chapter, I want to show you many of the techniques I have developed for creating light within my paintings.

A Night on the Town—
The New York Deli

Night scenes are exciting to me because most of the details are the lights themselves. The first of the images I want to explore is *The New York Deli* (Figure 1), a place in New York City that no longer exists. It was the last painting of a New York scene that I created before I moved from there to the West Coast.

The scene is captured at night. The brightly lit interior of the restaurant spills out onto the sidewalk.

1 *The New York Deli.*

I painted the sidewalk as if it were daytime (Figure 2). Each block in the concrete was selected and then stained with the Airbrush, Dodge, and Burn tools. The texture was done with the Add Noise filter.

After I completed all the blocks, I selected the entire area of the sidewalk and saved it to an alpha channel (Figure 3).

Look again at *The New York Deli*. Notice the difference in the colors of the two halos of light on the ground. Varying factors caused this. The one spilling from the doorway has a yellowish cast to it. This comes from a direct light, probably a fluorescent fixture, just above the doorway. The walls visible beyond the glass doors are beige. The light spilling onto the street is picking up the beige reflections and warming the color of the glow.

The other halo has a reddish cast to it. This reflection of light is larger than the one from the doorway. For one thing, the window is much larger than the doorway. Also, there are more light sources at work here: the bright lights from inside the restaurant and the many lights illuminating the window display, as well as spotlights blazing down from the sign above the restaurant. All of these contribute to the size of the halo visible on the ground. The reddish color comes from the contents of the window and the awnings above, which are primarily red. Creating these halos was relatively easy, considering that this image was created before layers were available in Photoshop.

From this point on, I will lie a bit for your sake. I find it so funny to remember the techniques I employed when this image was created. Photoshop has come a long way since then. To teach you what I did then would only serve to confuse you in your exploration of the program. So I will teach you how to create halos by using the tools and methods currently available. Trust me when I tell you that you're better off.

After creating a new, blank alpha channel, I turned on the eye icon for the RGB channels so that the area of the sidewalk was visible through the alpha channel. Then I used the Path tool (the Lasso tool can be substituted) to create the shape of the first light spill (Figure 4). I was careful to go beyond the edge of the building to make sure that the glow would be flush against the edge. The need for this will be apparent later on.

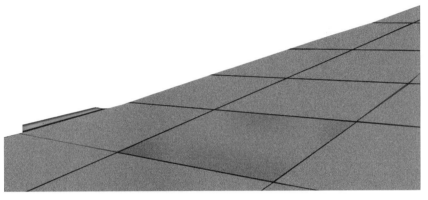

2 The area for the sidewalk was created as if it were being viewed by day, with all the detail necessary.

3 The entire area of the sidewalk was saved to an alpha channel.

4 To create the area for the light halo, I used the Path tool in an alpha channel.

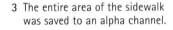

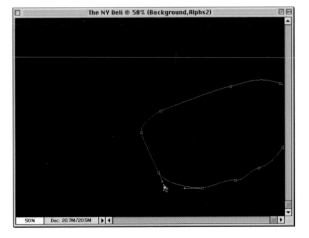

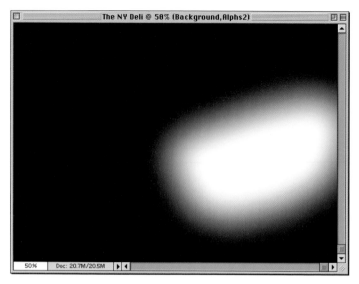

I turned the path into a selection with a large feather radius and then deleted this selected area from the alpha channel. That left a soft white halo in the channel (Figure 5).

To sharpen the edges of the light spill as it cascades off the sides of the window walls, I used the Airbrush tool with a brush shape that had a harder edge than the feather of the original selection (Figure 6). I used black for the color.

Using the Calculations dialog box, I subtracted the channel containing the overall shape of the sidewalk from the channel that contained the halo shape. The result of the calculation was sent to a new channel where the exposed area was the shape needed for the halo. Note in Figure 7 that the edge of the building is sharp and equal in value to the rest of the exposed area.

5 The selected area in the alpha channel was deleted, leaving a white halo effect.

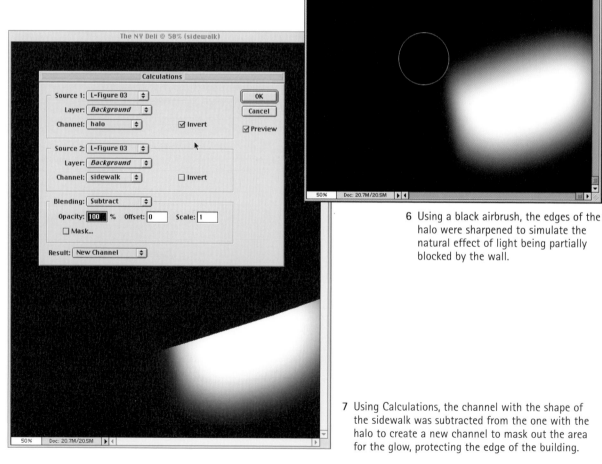

6 Using a black airbrush, the edges of the halo were sharpened to simulate the natural effect of light being partially blocked by the wall.

7 Using Calculations, the channel with the shape of the sidewalk was subtracted from the one with the halo to create a new channel to mask out the area for the glow, protecting the edge of the building.

8 The selected area in the image was colorized with the Hue/Saturation adjustment control to add the reddish tint to the sidewalk.

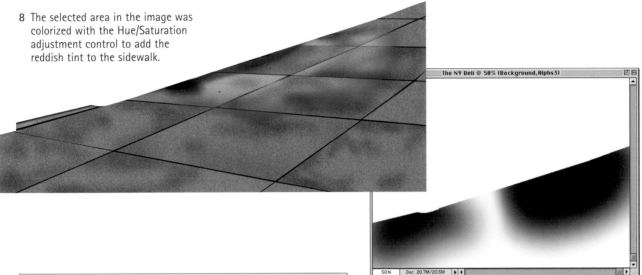

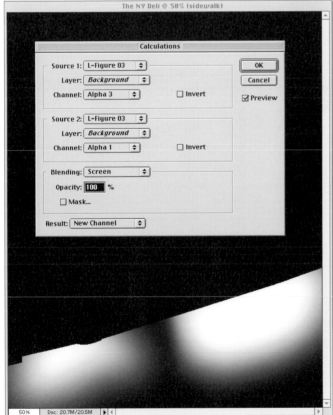

The NY Deli @ 50% (Background,Alphs3)

9 Using Calculations, the two channels with the shapes of the glows were screened together to form a new mask for the area of sidewalk not lit by light overflow.

The NY Deli @ 50% (sidewalk)

Calculations

Source 1: L-Figure 03
Layer: Background
Channel: Alpha 3   ☐ Invert

Source 2: L-Figure 03
Layer: Background
Channel: Alpha 1   ☐ Invert

Blending: Screen
Opacity: 100 %
☐ Mask...

Result: New Channel

OK
Cancel
☑ Preview

50% Doc: 20.7M/20.5M

10 The result of the calculations was sent to a new channel that was inverted to expose the unlit section of the sidewalk.

Back in the RGB color space, I loaded the alpha channel as a selection. Calling up the Hue/Saturation adjustment control, I chose the Colorize option to change the hue of the image while leaving the luminosity (lights and darks) untouched (Figure 8). I chose a hue that added the reddish tint I was looking for.

The same technique was employed to add the yellowish tint to the area in front of the doorway.

After the halos were completed, I created yet another alpha channel that combined the two halos into a single channel to expose the remaining area of the sidewalk. This was necessary to darken the sidewalk so that it had the effect of the darkness of night hiding the detail of the concrete.

Again, Calculations was brought into the act. I placed the two channels into Sources 1 and 2, and chose Screen for the Blending mode (Figure 9). This would ensure that the two channels were combined and blended evenly to create the proper mask for the balance of the unlit sidewalk.

I sent the result of the calculations to a new channel and then inverted the new channel (Figure 10) to reverse the exposure of the image that the alpha channel would select. I needed to expose the area of the sidewalk that was not being bathed with light.

I made the new alpha channel a selection and created a new layer to contain the shadow of night I was about to create. Then, using black as my color, I filled the selected area (Figure 11).

Okay, now I'm no longer lying.

Light spilling onto other surfaces in the image was handled in a much easier fashion. The awning just below the spotlights of the restaurant sign needed to show the light hitting it from above (Figure 12).

Using the same path that was used to create them, the awning edges were made into a selection. Then, with the Airbrush tool and a lighter-toned version of the color of the awning, I added a spray of color to the edge (Figure 13). Using a smaller brush shape and a very light tone, almost white, I added another spray of color to give the sense of the hot spot of light bouncing off the awning edge.

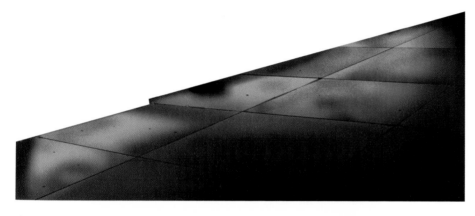

11 In a new layer, using black, I filled the selection made by the alpha channel. This gave me the shadows I needed to complete the effect of the darkness of night.

12 The awning above the restaurant shows a bounce off from the spotlight above.

13 Using the Airbrush tool, a highlight was added to the awning through a selection.

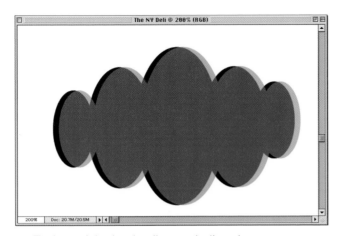

14 The layer of the door handles was duplicated and moved to the left of the original.

The light that reflected on the edges of the fancy door handles required a different technique. I duplicated the layer that contained the handles and then moved the layer with the handle in back to the left, to form an edge. In Figure 14, the original handle has been colored red and made transparent to demonstrate the shift in position for the duplicate. There was no color change for the actual handles in the painting.

Next, I selected Preserve Transparency for the layer and once again used the Airbrush tool. With white, I added small sprays of color to establish the light bouncing off the edges of the handles (Figure 15). Figure 16 shows the completed handles.

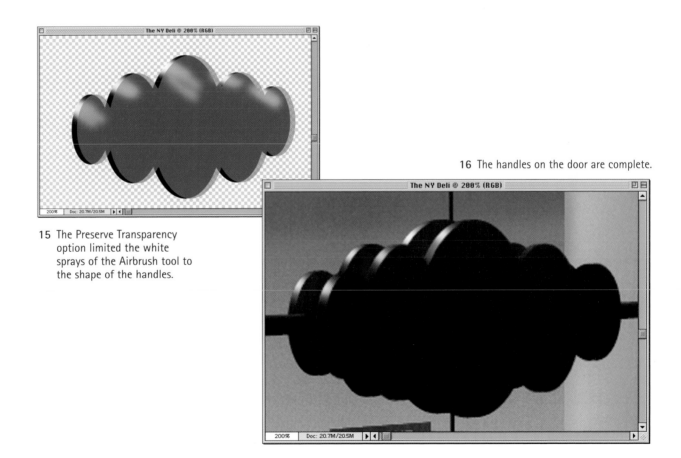

15 The Preserve Transparency option limited the white sprays of the Airbrush tool to the shape of the handles.

16 The handles on the door are complete.

A Night at the Movies—Hayden Orpheum

Hayden Orpheum is another night scene with a strong emphasis on light (Figure 17). This theater was across the street from the hotel where my wife and I stayed in Australia. The majority of the shapes visible in this image are the light sources themselves.

17 In this picture of the Hayden Orpheum, a theater in Australia, the neon marquee and store signs, plus the lit interiors of the stores, create most of the visible shapes.

18 The marquee has an arrangement of neon decorations that were created using the Blend tool in Illustrator.

Illustrator served as my main tool for creating all the elements in this image. The neon tubing on the main marquee was a series of blends (Figure 18).

In Illustrator, I created a simple line segment—a thick stroke with rounded endpoints—and colored it pink. This became the basis for the pink neon tubes. I duplicated the stroke and adjusted its size to represent one of the smaller tubes in the design. I took into account the perspective of the tubes as they descended over the edge of the marquee. Using the Blend tool, I created a blend from one stroke to the other with the appropriate steps to complete the neon design (Figure 19).

All of the line segments were imported into Photoshop as pixels because the colors and stroke weight had been applied in Illustrator. Now, a slight glow had to be added to complete the effect of bright neon tubes. (At the time I painted this image, I used the tubes to generate a feathered selection to create the glow.) With the current version of Photoshop, which at the time of the printing of this book is 5.5, it is easier to simply use the Outer Glow Layer Effect (Layer>Effects>Outer Glow) to generate the glow of the neon tubes (Figure 20). I selected a color similar to the color of the neon but lighter in value. I also increased the Blur factor. The higher the blur, the stronger the glow will appear.

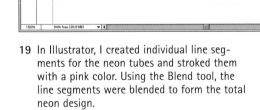

19 In Illustrator, I created individual line segments for the neon tubes and stroked them with a pink color. Using the Blend tool, the line segments were blended to form the total neon design.

20 Photoshop 5.5 can add the necessary glow to the neon.

21 A black airbrush was used to add dark tones to the ends of the neon tubes. The neon layer had Preserve Transparency selected to ensure that the strokes of the airbrush would be confined to the area of the tubes.

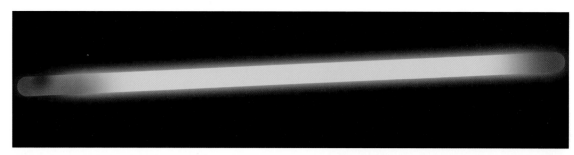

22 The name of the theater required a different approach. The letters were made of a translucent material with neon tubes within.

For that final touch of realism, I selected Preserve Transparency for the layer of the neon tubes so I could add that nasty little grime you see at the ends of old neon signs. Also, the far ends of the tubes are usually painted black to make a definite end to the shape of a letter within the glass tube of the neon sign. Using the Airbrush tool and black for my color, I added dabs of tone to the edges of the neon tubes (Figure 21).

The main title of the theater, visible along the wall, was made of large translucent letters lit from the inside by white neon lights (Figure 22). The effect of the neon needed to be very soft.

To create the shape of the letters, I used the Broadway font in Illustrator. The Create Outlines option turned the text into shapes that could be further manipulated to match the actual letters on the sign (Figure 23). I also needed to distort the letters to follow the perspective of looking down the street.

23 The letters were created as straight text in Illustrator. Create Outlines was then applied to convert the text into shapes that could be distorted to match the perspective of the scene.

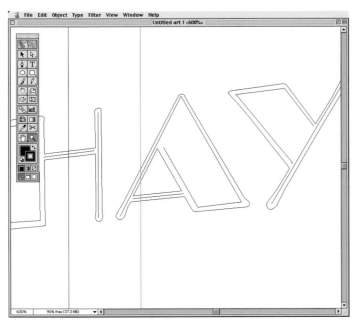

24 Paths were created for the neon tubes visible through the letter shapes.

When the distortion of the letters was accomplished, strokes were created inside the shapes of the letters to serve as the neon tubes, partially visible through the material of the letters (Figure 24).

When I completed all the paths in Illustrator, I imported them into Photoshop. This time, they were imported as paths.

Because the paths for the letters and neon tubes were created together, it was necessary to separate them. In Photoshop, each path would be used for a different purpose.

In the Paths palette, the imported path was saved and duplicated. In the duplicate, the paths for the letter shapes were deleted. Returning to the original path, the paths that represented the neon tubes were deleted.

In a new layer, I turned the path for the letter shapes into a selection, filled the selection with black, and then saved it to an alpha channel (Figure 25).

25 In a new layer, the paths for the letter shapes were turned into a selection and filled with black. The selection was also saved to an alpha channel.

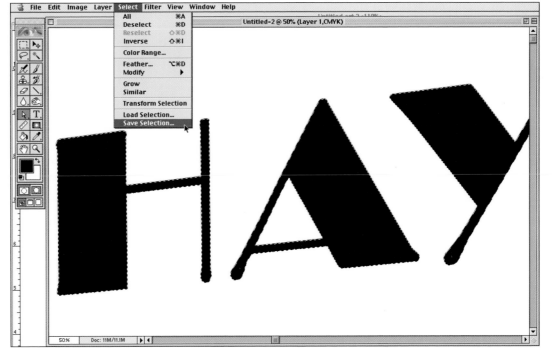

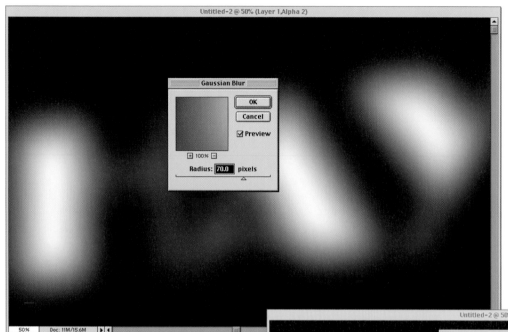

26 The duplicate channel was heavily blurred.

I duplicated the alpha channel and then, using the Gaussian Blur filter, heavily blurred the duplicate (Figure 26).

With the Calculations command, the original alpha channel of the letter shape was subtracted from the blurred channel (Figure 27). The result was sent to a new alpha channel that contained a very soft gradient, conforming to the shape of the letters and constrained to the shape of the letters themselves. This gradient was used to create the diffused glow that the translucent letters possess.

Turning the letter-glow alpha channel into a selection, I filled a new layer with a medium blue hue (Figure 28).

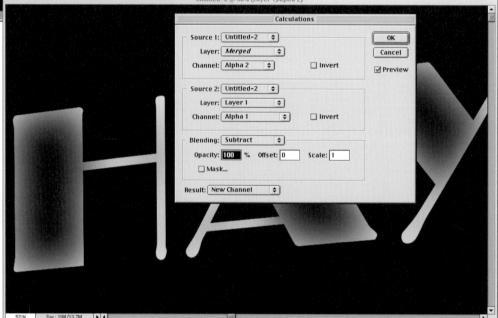

27 Using Calculations, a new channel was created where the original channel of the letter shapes was subtracted from the blurred channel.

In yet another layer, I stroked the paths for the tubes inside the letters with the Airbrush tool, using a soft-edged brush shape and a lighter version of the same blue.

This neon layer was blurred to further diffuse the edges (Figure 29).

The words "Picture Palace" underwent the same treatment, but with white used in place of blue for the words "Hayden Orpheum" (Figure 30). I used this same technique for other signs in the image (Figure 31).

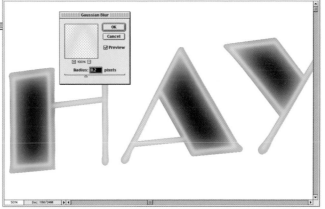

28 The new channel was turned into a selection and filled with a blue tone in a new layer.

29 The path for the neon tubes inside the letters was stroked and blurred to complete the effect.

30 The words below the theater name were created by using the same method.

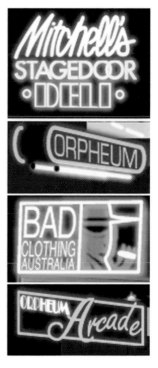

31 The various signs throughout the image were stroked paths with colored glows—the same technique used for the neon tubes of the marquee.

32 The image *Miller* is lit by a street light behind the tree on the left.

A Light Beyond—Miller

The image *Miller* is lit by a street light obstructed from view by a tree (Figure 32). The light is slightly visible through the foliage.

In the Background layer, a gradient of blue was applied with the Gradient tool. In a new layer, the light source was created using the Airbrush tool with different brush sizes and various shades of orange and white (Figure 33). I simply clicked once in the same spot with each brush shape. The shapes got progressively smaller as the color being used got lighter.

By clicking the eye icon in the Layers palette, I made visible the layer with the tree in front of the light source (Figure 34).

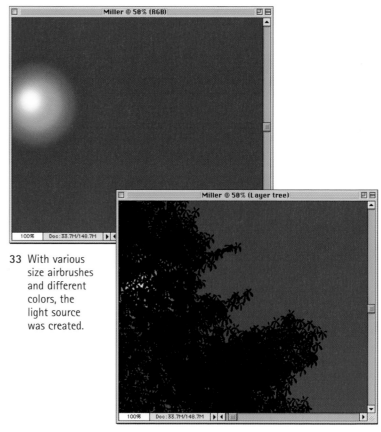

33 With various size airbrushes and different colors, the light source was created.

34 The layer with the tree in front of the light pole was made visible.

After duplicating the layer of the tree, I turned on that duplicate layer's Preserve Transparency option and filled the layer with an orange color that I felt matched the color of the glow visible on the leaves (Figure 35).

A layer mask was applied to the orange-colored tree layer (Figure 36), so that the light reflected on the leaves would seem to fade as it got farther away from the light source (Figure 37). I used a radial gradient for the effect.

I transferred the orange-colored layer to a position behind the layer of the black silhouetted tree. Then I offset it—up just a few pixels—so that it would be visible only at the edges of the black-tree layer, creating the impression of light reflections on the edges of the leaves (Figure 38).

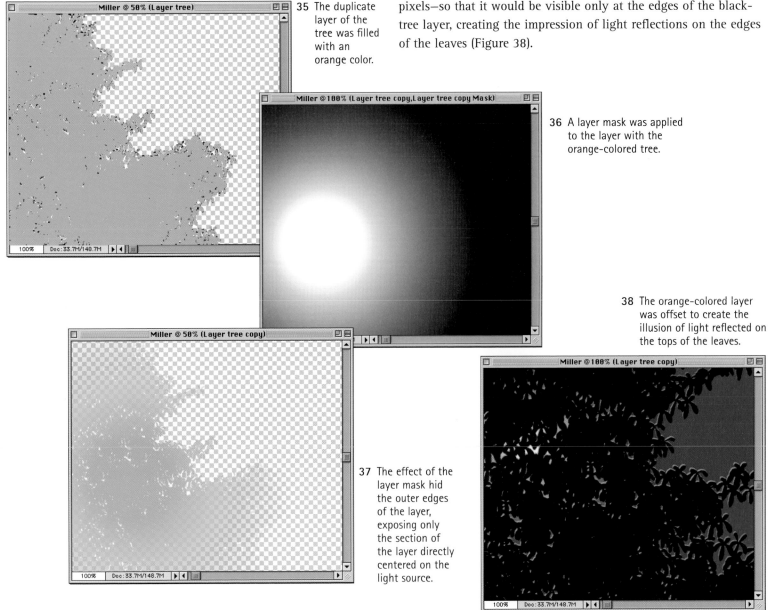

35 The duplicate layer of the tree was filled with an orange color.

36 A layer mask was applied to the layer with the orange-colored tree.

37 The effect of the layer mask hid the outer edges of the layer, exposing only the section of the layer directly centered on the light source.

38 The orange-colored layer was offset to create the illusion of light reflected on the tops of the leaves.

Reflected Light

Earlier in this chapter, you saw the creation of neon lights. I referred to them as "tubes." After all, that is what they are—glass tubes. When glass is illuminated, it acts as a light source by reflecting that light back. Later in the book, I have dedicated an entire chapter, Chapter 9, to reflections on surfaces. However, I think that now is a good time to discuss light reflections.

To create the highlights on the neon tubes, I set the brushes to Fade. Fade establishes the point at which the tool will run out of paint as you drag it over the image.

Neon Tubes—The Studio Theater

Rounded glass edges pick up light and concentrate it. The image *The Studio theater* has neon tubes all over its marquee (Figure 39). The scene was captured during the day, so the neon lights are off. (For that matter, they are off at night as well because the theater is abandoned.) The point is to show the way the neon tubes are picking up the sun.

The process by which these light reflections were created is something we can do together. Keep in mind that this is a technique, and it should not be limited to the creation of light reflections.

To begin, let me explain the process. To create the highlights on the neon tubes, I set the brushes to Fade. Fade establishes the point at which the tool will run out of paint as you drag it over the image.

The Fade amount is determined by the brush size and the spacing assigned to the brush. Both of these parameters are set in the Brush Options dialog box. If you set Fade to 20, the stroke will continue to lay down paint until 20 brush shapes have been laid down. In this example, I used the Airbrush tool for the stroke. To further understand the concept of Spacing within the context of the Tools options, try the following little exercise.

39 The neon tubes are picking up the sun's reflection, which causes sparkles on their edges.

© Bert Monroy 1999

Exercise 3.1 Stepping through Reflections

To create reflections of your own, follow these steps:

1 In Photoshop, start a new file that is 8 inches by 8 inches. Set the resolution to 72 pixels per inch (Figure 40).

2 Choose the Airbrush tool and the largest hard-edged, default brush shape (Figure 41).

3 In the Airbrush Options dialog box, set the Fade to 20 steps (Figure 42).

4 Make a single click in the upper-left corner of the canvas (Figure 43).

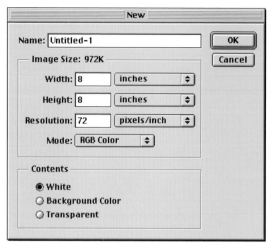

40 Start a new Photoshop file using these settings.

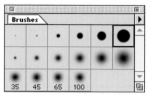

41 Choose the largest hard-edged brush shape.

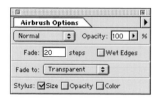

42 Set the fade to 20.

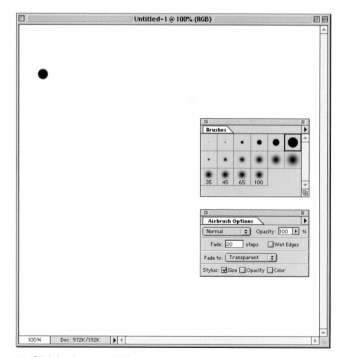

43 Click in the upper-left corner to make the first brush stroke.

5. Place the cursor on the right edge of the canvas and, with the Shift key pressed, click the mouse button (Figure 44).

6. Double-click on the brush in the Brushes palette, change the Spacing to 100% in the Brush Options dialog box that pops up (Figure 45), and click OK.

7. Place the cursor just below your original stroke and click (Figure 46).

8. Place the cursor over to the far right edge of the canvas and, with the Shift key pressed, click again (Figure 47).

Now you really have some action going on!

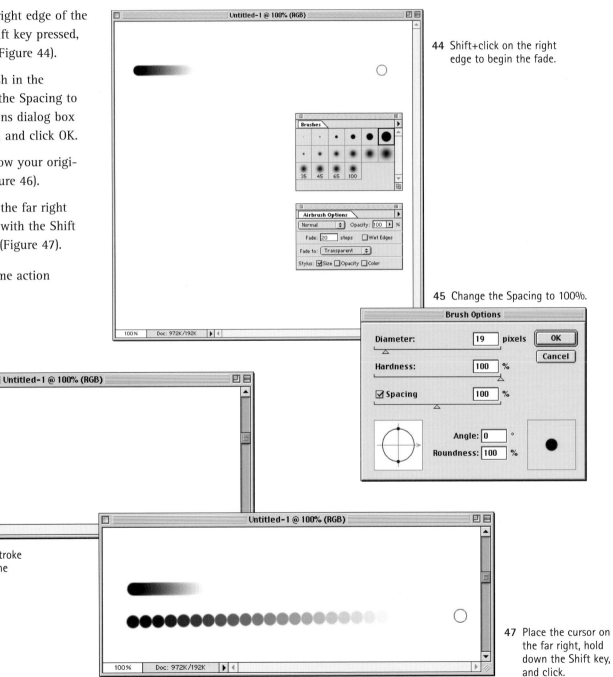

44 Shift+click on the right edge to begin the fade.

45 Change the Spacing to 100%.

46 Place the cursor under the stroke and click the beginning of the second stroke.

47 Place the cursor on the far right, hold down the Shift key, and click.

The second stroke is longer because the spacing is 100%. This means that, as the brush is dragged along the canvas, it lays down complete individual brush shapes that butt up against each other.

If the spacing is greater than 100%, there will be space between the brush shapes. With anything lower than 100%, the shapes blend into each other. The lower the spacing, the denser the line.

> **n o t e** | The point of pressing the Shift key is that it connects click to click as a straight line. Without pressing the Shift key, you have to depend on the steadiness of your hand to create a straight line.

There are additional options to Fade. It can be set to fade to transparent (the option I used) or to fade to the background color. The latter setting will use the foreground up to the point of fade out, lessening in opacity as the brush shape takes on the color of the currently selected background color. At that point, the tool will continue to apply a stroke, using the background color until the mouse button is released. Let's use the technique just outlined to create a sparkle effect.

Exercise 3.2   Stepping through a Sparkle

You can add a sparkle to just about anything if you follow these steps:

1 Open up any image you have of a person's face (Figure 48).

2 Make sure you have the Brush Size option selected in the Preferences dialog box (File>Preferences>Display & Cursors), as shown in Figure 49.

3 Choose a small, soft-edged brush. Compare it to the image and use a size about half the size of the person's pupil (Figure 50).

4 Choose white for your Foreground color.

48 Open an image of a person's face.

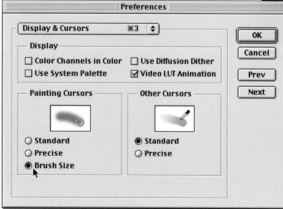

49 Select the Brush Size option in the Preferences dialog box.

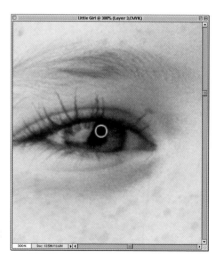

50 Choose a brush that is about half the size of the pupil.

5 Set the brush Fade to 20 steps (Figure 51).

6 Create a new layer to contain the sparkle (Figure 52).

7 Click once at the spot where you want the center of the sparkle to be (Figure 53).

8 Place the cursor up and far enough away from the first click to accommodate 20 steps. Remember that the second click is going to lead from the first, so place the cursor at the angle you want your sparkle to have (Figure 54).

9 With the Shift key pressed, click the mouse button (Figure 55).

   This should give you the first stroke of your sparkle. It should look similar to the one shown here. If it is too long or too short, adjust the fade out steps accordingly. If it is too big or too small, change your brush shape and repeat steps 1 through 9.

10 Release the Shift key and click on the center (original click) of the sparkle (Figure 56).

51 Set the Fade to 20.

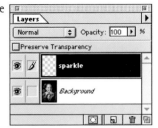

52 Place the sparkle on a new layer.

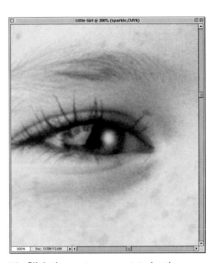

53 Click the spot you want to be the center of the sparkle.

54 Place the cursor at the correct angle.

55 Hold down the Shift key and click.

56 Click the same spot you clicked in Figure 53.

Exercise 3.2 Stepping through a Sparkle *(continued)*

11 Place the cursor far below at an angle that follows the line you created in the previous steps (Figure 57).

12 With the Shift key pressed, click the mouse button (Figure 58).

You have now completed the vertical streak for your sparkle.

n o t e | This is the exact technique I used to create the light reflections on the neon tubes of the theater marquee. The angles I used were dictated by the angle of the tubes. I simply Shift+clicked within the tubes.

13 Set the Fade to 10, half as many steps as before (Figure 59).

14 Release the Shift key and click on the center (original click) of the sparkle (Figure 60).

15 Place the cursor far to the left, at an angle perpendicular to the streak you have completed (Figure 61).

57 Place the cursor so that it continues the line you've begun.

58 Hold down the Shift key and click to finish the vertical part of the sparkle.

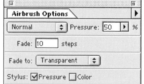

59 Set Fade to 10.

60 Release the Shift key and click on the center.

61 Place the cursor at the correct angle.

16 With the Shift key pressed, click the mouse button (Figure 62).

17 Release the Shift key and click on the center (original click) of the sparkle (Figure 63).

18 Place the cursor far to the right of the sparkle, at an angle that follows the line you created in steps 14 through 17 (Figure 64).

19 With the Shift key pressed, click the mouse button (Figure 65). There you have it! You've put a twinkle in your person's eye.

62 Hold down the Shift key and click.

63 Release the Shift key and click on the center.

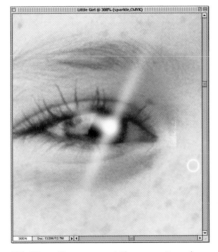

64 Place the cursor at the correct angle.

65 Hold down the Shift key and click. There's that sparkle.

More Reflected Light—
Clinique and a Doughnut

The bottle of nail enamel in Figure 66, an image commissioned by Clinique International, is picking up a light source along its edge. The sparkle of light on the bottle required a different technique than the one you just used—one for when the fading strokes of the reflection don't follow a straight line.

Liquids reflect light—and seldom in a straight line. Light reflected on a liquid will follow the edge, no matter what direction it takes. In the bottle image, the sparkle rides along a curved edge. The

glass bottle is a hard surface with a definite curve to the edge. Note, too, the jelly visible in the doughnut in Figure 67.

In these cases, it is vital to have control over the path the stroke follows. Oops! I gave you the answer! The Path tool.

Any path generated with the Path tool can be stroked with any of the other tools in Photoshop. I mentioned that very idea at the beginning of this chapter, when we used the Path tool to create neon. The difference here is that the strokes will fade out.

66 The edge of the bottle is picking up a glimmer of light.

67 The sheen on the jelly oozing out of the doughnut makes it look wet.

The one major consideration in using this technique is that the stroke follows the direction in which the path was created. To create a sparkle like those in the jelly and the bottle, I had to create two separate paths in opposing directions. The first path was created going left to right (Figure 68).

The second path went from right to left (Figure 69). Then, they were placed so that the starting points butted up against each other (Figure 70). They must remain separate paths for the effect to work properly.

I then chose the Airbrush, color, and brush size. I stroked the paths, and the Fade took effect on both sides, making a continuous shimmer of light (Figure 71).

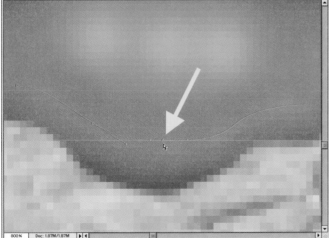

68 The first path was created in one direction.

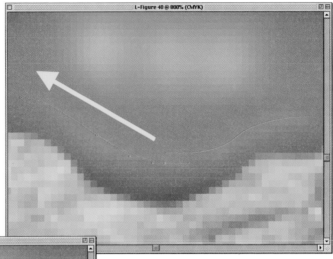

69 The second path was created in the opposite direction from the first.

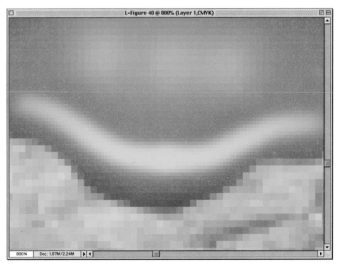

70 The two paths were positioned with the starting point of one resting on that of the other.

71 The result of stroking the paths is a continuous shimmer of light.

chapter 4

Shading

Shadows add life and dimension to any image, and without them, an object appears flat. By shading a scene properly, you give it the illusion of a third dimension. Unless, of course, the image isn't lit on all sides by gigantic spotlights—in which case, you enter a whole new realm of problems.

Watch any old Hitchcock movie, *Citizen Kane,* or any other great black-and-white movie. What you will see is a strong play of lights and shadows that add drama. Good lighting techniques made up for the lack of color and brought the audience into the scene. Likewise, the play of lights and shadows should be a strong consideration in creating a still image.

Both Illustrator and Photoshop are two-dimensional programs. Illustrator deals with vectors or coordinates that relate to an object's attributes and position on a page. Photoshop's files are configurations of a given number of pixels across and down. The third dimension is mimicked through the use of shading and perspective.

Lights and shadows determine the relationship of one object to another and their places within the total scene. The position and strength of the lights and shadows also set the overall mood of an image.

Figures 1 and 2 show the same image, which was rendered using a 3D program with two different lighting configurations. Figure 1, the brightly lit image, shows the bottle of wine in what could be a lively, lunchtime setting. In Figure 2, the setting could be a candlelit dinner for two. The only difference between the two images is the lighting, which creates two entirely different moods.

When you're compositing multiple objects into one scene, it is crucial that the lighting for each object matches correctly. Even an untrained eye will be able to spot a discrepancy. For instance, an object sitting under a lamp cannot have a shadow on its top. The light intensity and color must match—as well as the direction from which the light is emanating.

1 This brightly-lit scene gives the impression of a lunchtime meeting.

2 The same scene, but with subdued lighting, gives the impression of a candlelit dinner for two.

When you study Figure 3, you will notice a discrepancy in the lighting conditions for the overall scene. Notice the strong sunlight hitting the woman with the bag of groceries in the foreground. Here the sun is somewhere to the right. The background is very sunny also, but the sun appears to be coming from the left. The second woman, standing with hands on hips, is in a totally different, subdued lighting scheme.

Among the many factors to take into account when creating lighting effects for your scene are the following:

- The number of light sources
- The position of the light sources
- The strength of the lights
- The color of the lights
- Other objects blocking the light
- The material(s) of which objects in the scene are made

Figures 4 through 9 are examples of the effects light can have on objects, or how they cast shadows onto other objects.

The position of the light source affects the length of the shadow cast. The lower the light source (the closer it is to the horizon), the longer the shadow will appear. A tree in a meadow at sunset will cast a long shadow (Figure 4).

The higher the light source, the shorter the shadow. The same tree, in the late morning, will cast a shorter shadow (Figure 5).

3 In this composite, lighting of the elements was not considered.

5 The sun is higher so the shadow is shorter.

4 The sun is relatively low so the shadow is longer.

81

A light source directly above an object will cast little to no shadow, depending on the shape of the object. At noon, the tree casts a shadow directly below it (Figure 6).

When shadows are cast against another object, the shape and position of the second object will affect the shadow's shape.

In Figure 7, you see a shadow being cast along the floor and up a wall. The wall facing the object is perpendicular to the light source. The effect is a continuation of the shadow up the wall. The slight decrease in the size of the shadow in relation to the size of the cylinder is caused by the fact that the wall is farther away than the cylinder.

Figure 8 has the wall angled away from the light source. Notice that the shadow seems to get thicker. This is due to the fact that the shadow travels in a straight line and crosses the wall at an angle. The box at the bottom further illustrates this point.

The first diagram in Figure 9 shows the positions of the light source, object, and wall in Figure 7. Notice the short shadow. The second diagram in Figure 9 shows how elongated the shadow becomes when the angle of the wall changes.

6 Because the light source is directly above the object, the shadow is small.

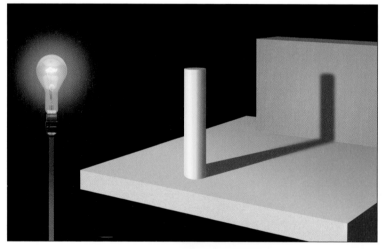

7 The shadow is being cast along the floor and up a wall. The wall faces the object in a direction perpendicular to the light source.

8 The wall is angled away from the light source, which makes the shadow seem to get thicker.

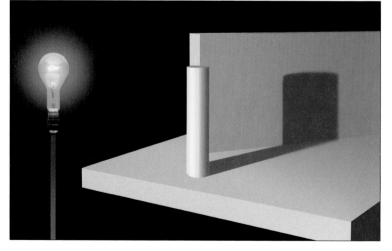

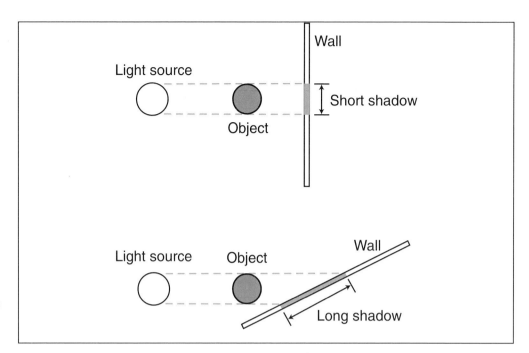

9 These two diagrams show the effect the angle of the wall has on the shadow.

The Drop Shadow

The shadow cast by one object against another—the *drop shadow*—has become a staple of computer graphics (Figure 10). So widespread is its use that Photoshop has incorporated it as a menu option.

Before the introduction of layers, the process of creating drop shadows was achieved through an elaborate assortment of Calculation and alpha-channel techniques. Photoshop 3 gave us layers, which simplified the creation of drop shadows.

10 Here you see a piece of text casting a drop shadow on the background.

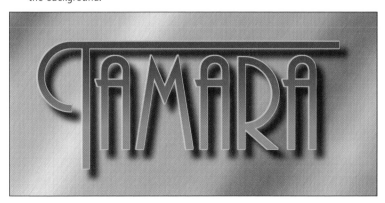

Photoshop 5 introduced the Drop Shadow layer effect, resident in the layer's menu. This feature automates the process previously achieved with multiple layers. Why don't you try your hand with the effect and join me in a little exercise?

Exercise 4.1   Stepping through Drop Shadow Effects

To get the Drop Shadow effect, follow these steps:

1 Select the layer that will cast the shadow and choose the Drop Shadow function (Layer>Effects>Drop Shadow) (Figure 11).

   Figure 12 shows the dialog box that pops up when you activate the Drop Shadow feature. This box gives you full control over the following attributes (which you can modify at any time after the fact by clicking on the effects' icon in the Layers palette) of the shadow:

   - The Color for the shadow. Different colored lights affect the color of the shadow they cast.

   - The Mode, or the way the shadow interacts with the layers below the shadow layer. These mode controls are identical to those found in Photoshop's layers and tools. Refer to your manual for a more detailed description.

   - The Opacity, or transparency, added to the shadow.

   - The Angle at which the shadow is cast from the object creating it.

   - The Distance from the object. This distance determines the spatial relationship of the object casting the shadow to the background on which the shadow is being cast.

   - The Blur factor, or the softening of the edges of the shadow. A strong spotlight creates a sharp-edged shadow. Candlelight produces a soft-edged shadow.

   - The Intensity, or strength, of the shadow effect. This intensity is more like the strength of the light producing the shadow. A higher value increases the effect.

   The resulting shadow becomes part of the layer that contains the object casting the shadow. In the Layers palette, the layer is marked as containing an effect.

2 Choose Layer>Effects>Create Layer to place the drop shadow into its own layer (Figure 13), making available many additional effects, such as Displacement. (The Displacement effect on shadows is discussed later in this chapter.)

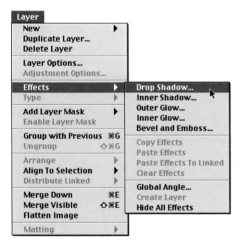

11 Choose Drop Shadow from a submenu option of Photoshop's Layer menu.

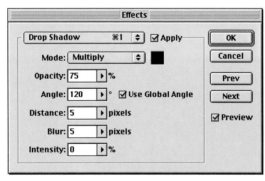

12 Set the attributes in the Effects dialog box that pops up when you invoke the feature, giving you full control over the shadow's attributes.

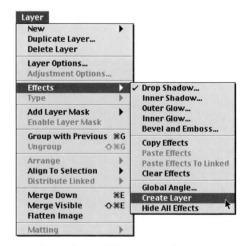

13 Choose Layer>Effects>Create Layer to separate the Drop Shadow into its own layer.

Shadow Effects

Taking into account what has been discussed so far, let's see how I have applied these concepts to my images.

In the image entitled *Cedar*, one of the more difficult effects I tried to create was the shadow of the tree sweeping across the wall (Figure 14). The shadow is long because the light source, the setting sun, is low on the horizon.

Using Multiple Layers

Because it is the tree that is casting the shadow, the tree itself is used to create the shadow. The tree trunk and all the leaves were created in multiple layers that were merged together into a single layer after the tree was complete. This procedure is outlined in further detail in Chapter 6, "Creating a Greener World."

14 *Cedar.*

digital masters | bert monroy

The layer that contained the merged tree was duplicated by dragging it over the Make New Layer icon at the bottom of the Layers palette (Figure 15).

I turned on Preserve Transparency for the layer so that only the tree and leaves would be affected (Figure 16). It was then filled with black. This black layer would serve as the basis for the shadow.

> **n o t e** | Preserve Transparency allows you to modify only the pixels in the layer that are active. The transparent area of the layer will maintain its transparency.

Then I turned off Preserve Transparency so that I could apply a Blur filter to soften the shadow.

> **n o t e** | The Blur filters create their effect inward and outward from the edge of the object being blurred. A Gaussian Blur of 10 softens the edge 5 pixels inward and 5 outward. Thus, when Preserve Transparency is turned on, the effect doesn't work properly.

Using the Scale tool (Edit>Transform>Scale), I stretched the black tree to the width of the entire image (Figure 17). This achieved the effect of a long shadow across the wall.

The shadow is basically a darkening of the underlying layers. To get this effect, the mode for the layer was changed to Multiply so that the black would have the effect of darkening the existing colors of the layers underneath. When a layer is set to Multiply, it actually multiplies its pixels' brightness values with those of the layers below it. This significantly darkens the layers beneath.

15 When you drag a layer over the Make New Layer icon, you duplicate the layer.

16 With Preserve Transparency turned on for the layer, it was filled with black.

17 Using the Scale tool, the black tree was stretched to the width of the entire image.

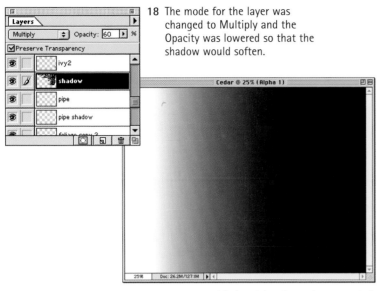

18 The mode for the layer was changed to Multiply and the Opacity was lowered so that the shadow would soften.

Finally, the Opacity was lowered so that the shadow would soften (Figure 18).

Because the shadows are long and cast against a wall at an angle, this shadow must blur out more at the outer edges than in the area immediately behind the tree. It will also appear to stretch as it gets further from the source. To achieve this effect, I created an alpha channel with a horizontal gradient from white to black (Figure 19).

I made the alpha channel a selection and applied a Motion Blur filter to the layer of the shadow (Figure 20). The result was the desired effect of a stretched and blurred shadow being cast by the tree across the wall (Figure 21).

As the shadow moves farther from the source, ambient light lightens the intensity of a shadow. To achieve this effect, I applied a layer mask (Figures 22 and 23).

19 An alpha channel was created, with a horizontal gradient from white to black.

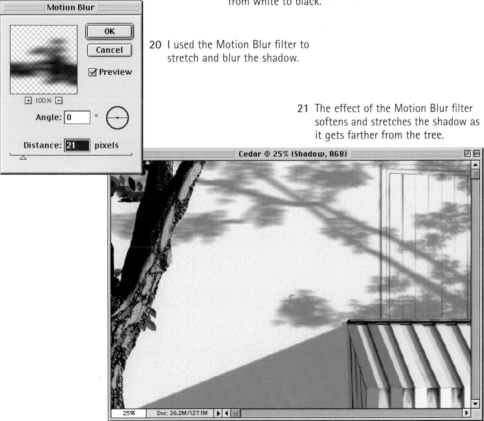

20 I used the Motion Blur filter to stretch and blur the shadow.

21 The effect of the Motion Blur filter softens and stretches the shadow as it gets farther from the tree.

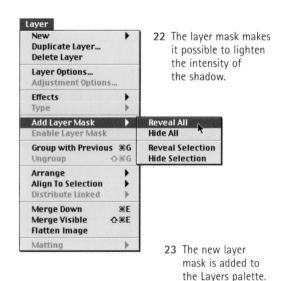

22 The layer mask makes it possible to lighten the intensity of the shadow.

23 The new layer mask is added to the Layers palette.

In a layer mask, black hides the contents of the layer; white allows the contents to be seen. I didn't want the shadow to totally disappear, so a gradient I created in the layer mask was gray-to-white rather than black-to-white (Figure 24).

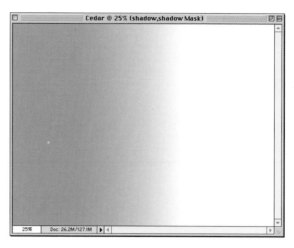

24 I created a gray-to-white gradient in the layer mask.

Using the Path Tool

The shadow being cast by the awning was created in its own layer by using the Path tool in Photoshop (Figure 25). This is the procedure with which I achieve most of the shadows in my paintings.

With the Path tool, I generate the shape for the shadow. It is then turned into a selection and filled with black. The layer is then blurred with the Gaussian Blur filter. Finally, the opacity is lowered. (The settings for the filter and opacity vary from image to image. The determining factors are based on the intensity of the light on the scene.)

Figures 26 through 28 show another example of how to use the Path tool to make shapes for the shadows.

I then imported the path into Photoshop, turned it into a selection, and filled it with black and blurred it to complete the shadow.

25 The shadow being cast by the awning was created in its own layer with the Path tool.

© Bert Monroy 1994

26 The painting *Akihabara* is of a corner in the electronics district of Tokyo.

27 Zooming into the area of the scooter, you can see the shadow it casts on the ground.

28 The shadow being cast by the scooter was created with the Path tool in Illustrator.

Shadows on Angled Surfaces

Shadows that fall upon angled surfaces distort to follow the angle(s). In the image *Rendez-vous*, a series of shadows add drama and give a sense of the time of day (Figure 29).

Zooming in on the section of the sign on the sidewalk, you can see the play of shadows caused by the chain (Figure 30).

As with the layer of the tree in the previous example, the layer of the chain was duplicated and filled with black to serve as the shadow layer. This shadow layer was duplicated several times because the shadow falls on different elements in the image. Each new element has its own angle.

The first of the duplicated layers required the shadow to be skewed downward with the Skew function (Edit>Transform>Skew) (Figure 31).

29 *Rendez-vous.*

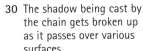

30 The shadow being cast by the chain gets broken up as it passes over various surfaces.

31 The shadow layer has been skewed downward.

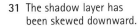

It was then scaled down on the horizontal to make it thinner. The fact that the wooden post on which the shadow is being cast is at an angle to the light source causes a shrunken effect on the shadow. To show the shadow only within the area of the wooden post, the layer of the shadow and the layer of the sign were made into a clipping group.

On the lower support bar of the sign, two shadows were added (Figure 32). The first was straight, for the upper edge of the board. The second went through the same transformation as the one on the upper post.

The final shadow on the sidewalk was simply scaled down to make it smaller (Figure 33). A slight Blur filter was applied to soften it. The setting you use will vary, depending on how soft you want the shadow to be. The farther from the object casting the shadow, the softer the shadow becomes.

The larger shadow caused by a tree outside the viewer's field of view went through the same transformations as the chain.

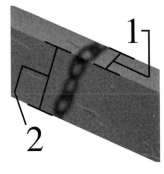

32 I made the shadow marked 1 straight, but I transformed the shadow marked 2.

33 The shadow on the sidewalk was scaled down to make it smaller, and a Blur filter was applied to soften it.

Multiple Light Sources

The image *marble and matches* introduces a new interaction of light and shadow–two light sources (Figure 34). This interaction is evident just under the match that is leaning against the matchbox.

The first is a light source from above, just slightly to the rear of the objects. It is the stronger of the two, as you can see from the strength of the shadow cast to the front of the objects.

The second light source, from the front and to the left, casts a softer, lighter shadow. At the point where the two shadows intersect (at the lower front edge of the matchbox), the area becomes darker.

The shadow of the matchstick that is leaning against the matchbox is going through an additional transformation. Because the matchstick is leaning away from the surface, the shadow gets softer as it gets farther away from the match (Figure 35). This is the same behavior you saw in the shadow of the tree at the beginning of this chapter.

I selected the area where the shadow falls (Figure 36) and then saved the selection to an alpha channel (Figure 37). I turned the alpha channel into a selection and, in the alpha channel itself, laid down a gradient to give the strongest effect at the point in the shadow that is farthest away (Figure 38). Then, I applied a Blur filter through the channel onto the shadow.

34 *marble and matches.*

35 Because the matchstick that is leaning up against the matchbox is leaning away from the surface, it requires an additional transformation.

36 I selected the area where the shadow falls.

37 This selection became an alpha channel.

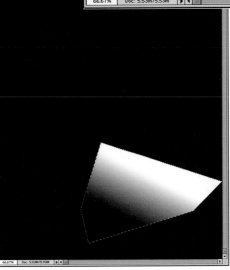

38 The gradient in the alpha channel is strongest at the point in the shadow that is farthest away.

Transparency and Shadows

So far, you have seen the effect of shadows cast by solid, opaque objects. These lighting effects are fairly predictable. The beginning of this chapter explains the physics involved, which are not very complicated. By following the techniques I already have shown you, you will be able to duplicate the effects of shadows with little effort.

Now we shall explore a more complicated sort of shading—the shadows cast by objects that are not opaque.

The Marble

The marble in the image *marble and matchsticks* required some additional effects for its shadow. The marble is made of transparent blue glass through which light passes. The density of the material will hold back some transference of light, however, and its color will affect the color of the shadow.

The overall shadow for the marble was the first thing to be created. In a layer created specifically for the shadow, an elliptical shape was selected with the Elliptical Marquee Tool. The selection was feathered to soften the edge (Figure 39). It was then filled with a dark blue.

I used black to create the shadow of the other objects because they totally block the passage of light. But, as mentioned earlier, the marble is transparent blue glass and allows some light to pass through, so its shadow is dark blue. The light passes through the blue glass and is colored by it, but it is partially blocked by the dense nature of the glass.

My next step was to create the blue haze caused by the refracted light. To do this, I selected a narrower oval within the area of the marble's shadow (Figure 40) and saved the oval as a selection into an alpha channel (Figure 41).

Another oval, narrower than the last one, was selected, saved as a channel, and blurred heavily (Figure 42). Using the Calculations command, the blurred channel was subtracted from the original alpha channel (Figure 43). This gave me a mask that would increase the softness of the effect inward, toward the center of the oval (Figure 44).

39 In a new layer, an oval was selected with a slight feather to the edges.

40 A narrow oval was selected within the area of the marble's shadow.

41 The selected oval was saved as a selection into an alpha channel, and blurred.

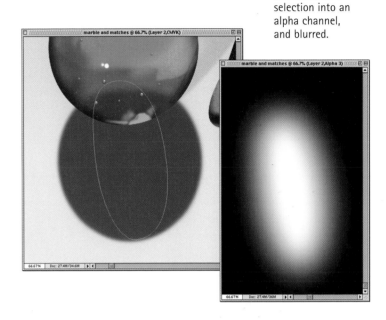

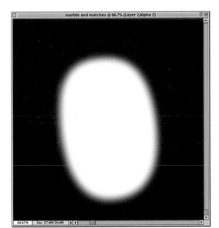

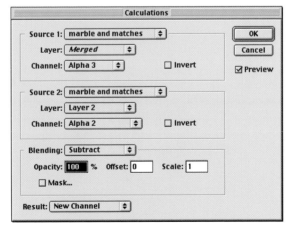

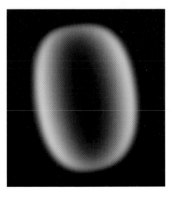

42 Another narrower oval was created, saved to an alpha channel, and blurred heavily.

43 Using the Calculations command, I subtracted the narrowest heavily blurred channel from the original narrow alpha channel. The results were sent to a new channel.

44 The Calculations result gave me a mask that would increase the softness of the effect inward, toward the center of the oval.

95

The results were sent to a new channel. This final channel was then blurred again to soften the overall effect (Figure 45).

Back in the RGB channels, a new layer was created. The channel was made into a selection and filled with a lighter blue than the one previously used to create the shadow (Figure 46).

The highlights visible within the shadow were created with the Airbrush tool, using various shades of light blue and white (Figure 47).

46 I filled the selected channel with a lighter shade of blue than the one I used to create the shadow.

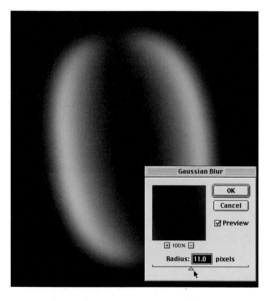

45 The final channel was blurred to soften the overall effect.

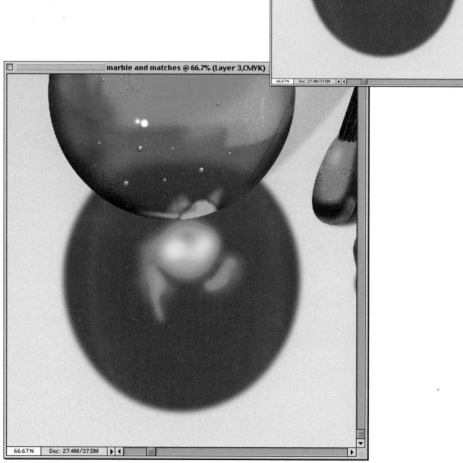

47 I used the Airbrush tool to create the highlights you can see in the shadow.

The Clear Glass Ointment Applicator

Another example of light traveling through transparent objects can be seen in the image *ointment*, where the shadow of the glass applicator runs across the cork (Figure 48). The applicator is made of clear glass, so colorization of the shadow wasn't necessary.

In this case, the light passing through the cylindrical shape of the applicator was amplified. The applicator acted as a magnifying glass, concentrating the light in a bright streak.

To create this effect, I employed the Paintbrush tool. I set the brush to *fade out* (run out of paint) at a given point (Figure 49), and I created a new layer to house the highlight.

n o t e | If you hold down the Shift key while you're using any of the tools, you get a straight line from click to click.

With the Shift key down, I clicked with the Paintbrush tool at the base where the highlight began, and then again at the other end of the top of the cork, following the direction of the shadow. The result was light shining through the glass applicator (Figure 50).

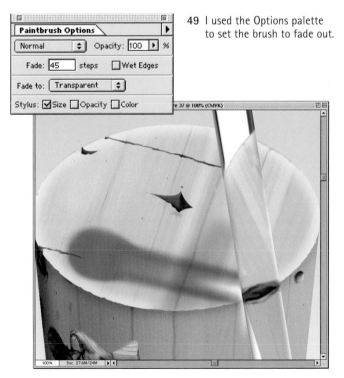

49 I used the Options palette to set the brush to fade out.

50 Can you see the light shining through the glass applicator?

48 *ointment.*

97

Colored Shadows

As you have seen in the previous examples, the color of the shadow can be affected by a variety of situations. In the case of the marble, its material affected the color of the light passing through it.

Another variable that affects a shadow's attributes is the color of the light source itself. The image *Verbum Be-In 8* was commissioned for a poster announcing a Digital Be-In event (Figure 51). The client wanted a Mobius strip in a circuslike setting, with colored spotlights hitting it from all sides. The shadows cast from these light sources would take the shape of the figure 8.

When an object is lit from several sides, the resulting shadows will affect each other. You saw the result of two light sources on the background in the previous image of *marble and matches*.

This image not only has multiple light sources, but it also has multiple colors for the lights.

To create the paths that would make up the Mobius strip (Figure 52), I used Illustrator.

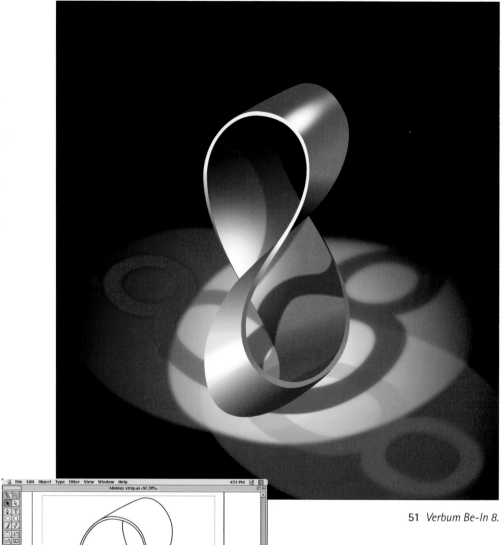

51 *Verbum Be-In 8.*

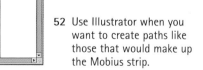

52 Use Illustrator when you want to create paths like those that would make up the Mobius strip.

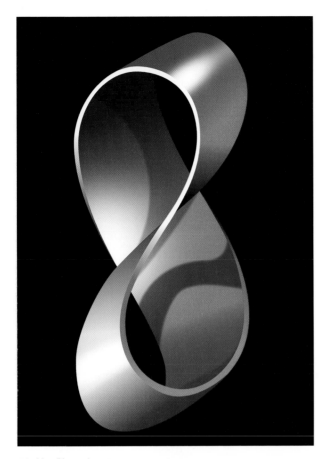

53 Use Photoshop to fill paths with various gradients.

I imported the paths into Photoshop, converted them into selections, and filled them with various gradients (Figure 53).

The shadow shapes were actual font-type number 8s that were blurred and skewed to fall onto the background.

To determine what color the shadows would take, I had to do some research. Before the computer came into my life, I generally had to construct elaborate sets, lit with colored gel-covered lights, to study the effects. The computer has simplified this process.

I turned to a 3D program to create the study (Figure 54). Due to the abstract nature of the image itself, I could not create the image in a 3D program.

I created some simple objects, added light sources that were colored the way I needed, and positioned them to hit the objects from the directions required for the poster scene. The program computed the results and gave me a reference from which to choose the colors I needed.

Using the Eyedropper tool, I chose colors from the file of the 3D image to fill the distorted numbers.

When this particular image was created, layers were not a feature in Photoshop. The overlapping shadow effects were achieved through an intricate series of Calculation commands that separated the areas where the shadows overlapped.

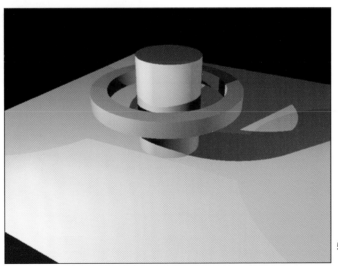

54 I used a 3D program to create the study.

In the versions of Photoshop since the introduction of layers, this process has been greatly simplified. Today, each distorted number 8 would be colored and blurred in its own layer. By changing the mode for the individual layers, I can get the desired results of overlapping colors.

Shadow Displacement

Shadows cast onto rough or textured back-drops must be distorted by that texture to look believable.

The image shown in Figure 55 demon-strates the effect the shadow of a bottle goes through when it is cast across a desert of rippled sand. The ripples in the sand distort the shadow along its edges.

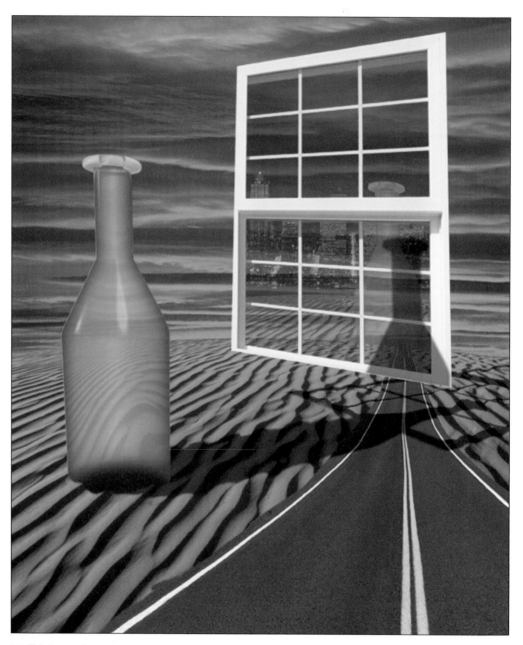

55 This image demonstrates the effect a shadow goes through when it is cast across a rippled texture.

100

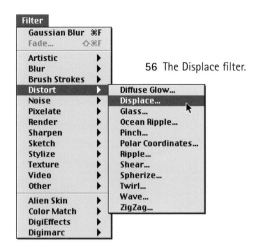

56 The Displace filter.

This effect is achieved with the use of the Displace filter (Figure 56). The Displace filter offsets pixels of one image based on the luminosity values of another.

The image used to displace another is called the *displacement map*. It takes white or light tonal values of the map file to offset the target pixels up and to the left. Black or dark tones will move the target pixels down and to the right. A 50% gray equals no displacement.

Duplicating the layer of the bottle and window frame created the shadow. I filled the layer with black, and then blurred and skewed it (Figure 57).

The Displace filter was selected. When the filter is applied, a dialog box appears in which you can set parameters for the effect (Figure 58). When you click OK, an additional dialog box appears that asks for the displacement map (Figure 59).

The image of the desert existed as a separate file. When the filter asked for a displacement map, the Desert file was used.

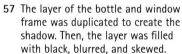

57 The layer of the bottle and window frame was duplicated to create the shadow. Then, the layer was filled with black, blurred, and skewed.

58 When the Displace filter is applied, a dialog box appears; in it, you can set parameters for the effect.

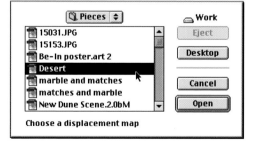

59 The file of the desert was selected.

The final effect shows the shadow, distorted to follow the ripples in the sand (Figure 60).

Notice that, due to the flat nature of the road, the area where the shadow crosses the road didn't require a displacement.

After I created the original shadow layer, I then duplicated it for the displacement effect. I left the original shadow layer that was not displaced in its unfiltered state and clipped it with the layer of the road, as seen in Figure 61.

> **n o t e** | To turn the layers into a clipping group, you hold down the Option key (the Alt key on a PC) and click between two layers in the Layers palette.

The transparency information of the bottom-most layer acts as a mask for the layers above it in the clipping group. I then placed these clipping grouped layers above the displaced shadow, thus giving the effect of a shadow's journey over the terrain. The displaced shadow rippled by the sand and the flat (original) shadow over the flat road.

In the next chapter, "Distorting with Displace," I get into more detail about this incredibly powerful filter.

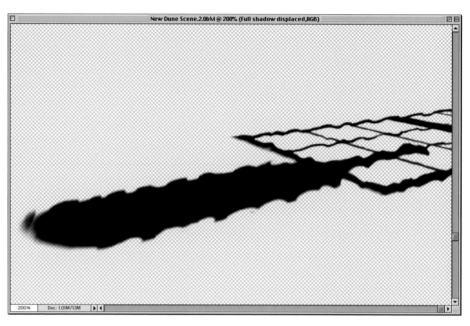

60 The final effect—a distorted shadow that follows the ripples in the sand

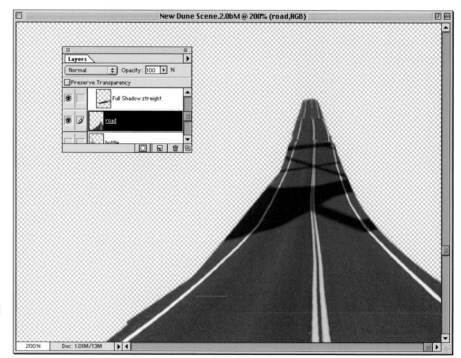

61 The layer of the road and the layer of the shadow became a clipping group.

chapter 5

Distorting with Displace

During my years lecturing around the world, I've heard many complaints that Photoshop lacks the capability to bend or distort images along user-defined curves. It just so happens that that capability has always been there: It's a filter that simply needs to be understood—the Displace filter.

In the chapter on shading, I ended with a little example of the use of this filter. I have decided to wedge this tiny chapter into the body of the book to further explore the many uses of this filter.

The Displace filter works with two files. The first is the image you want to distort and the second, the image used to distort it. The filter uses the *luminosity values* (lights and darks) of one image to distort the other.

White or light values distort an image up and to the left. Black or dark values distort an image down and to the right. A 50% gray value has no *displacement* (distortion). Keeping these facts in mind, you can create elaborate displacement maps to distort images in every way imaginable.

I resort to using the Displace filter many times during the creation of one of my paintings.

Coffee to Go

If you look closely at the image *Rendez-vous* in Figure 1, you will notice text that bends with the folds of the fabric of the awning. Of course, this being a book over which I have a bit of control, I'll make it easy for you to see that text. Don't look closely; I'll just provide you with a close-up (Figure 2). That is, after all, one of the features that drew me to the computer in the first place—the capability to zoom in and see details.

Looking at the image at an early stage of production (Figure 3), you can see that the awning is missing all the text.

1 *Rendez-vous*

© Bert Monroy 1999

2 Notice that the letters on the awning bend with the folds of the fabric.

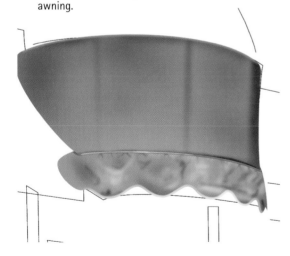

3 In this early version of the image, text is missing from the awning.

COFFEES

4 I created the text in its own layer, using the Text tool.

COFFEES

5 The individual letters were distorted to follow the perspective of the awning.

The text was created as straight text in Photoshop (Figure 4). I selected a font that closely matched the one that appeared on the actual awning. The text fell into its own completely editable layer as text because whenever you use the Text tool in Photoshop, the resulting text automatically falls into its own layer.

You can perform certain functions such as making a text layer a clipping group, but you can't distort or filter the layer. To perform these operations, you have to render the text layer. When the text layer is rendered, you can manipulate the individual characters because the text is no longer text but a pixelated visual of the text. What happens is that Photoshop releases the text so that it becomes a picture element. And a picture element's pixels can be manipulated in any way possible within Photoshop.

With the text on the awning, I selected each individual letter. Then, using the Distort function (Edit>Transform>Distort), the individual letters were distorted to simulate the wraparound of the text on the awning (Figure 5). They were twisted downward and also scaled down toward the inside to give the impression of fading back in perspective. (You did read the chapter on perspective, right?) The letters were then put in position around the edge of the awning.

At this point, I needed to create the displacement map, the file that the filter would use to distort the image. I created an alpha channel in which to create my map (Figure 6). (See Chapter 1 for more information on creating an alpha channel.) This allowed me to draw my map within the image itself, which was necessary for proper positioning. The fact that the creation of the map was restricted to the alpha channel also ensured that the image wouldn't be altered.

I filled the alpha channel with a 50% gray (Figure 7). Over this gray, I later added lighter tones to make the distortion. The gray guaranteed that the rest of the image wouldn't be distorted.

With the Airbrush tool, I then proceeded to create small wisps of light tones that would bend my text where I wanted it bent (Figure 8).

Now I needed to make the contents of the alpha channel into a file that could be used as a displacement map image. It needed to be a separate file, other than the one being distorted. (It would be nice if the Displace filter gave you the option to choose a particular channel of an image, but it doesn't. It looks for the image itself.)

Because the majority of the files I work on are large storage sizes, I usually don't depend on Copy and Paste to transfer image data. In the case of the alpha channel, I made it into a selection. I chose Select>Save Selection and saved it to a new document. This works faster than if I were to copy it and paste it into a new

6 I created an alpha channel where the displacement map would be created.

7 The channel was filled with a 50% gray.

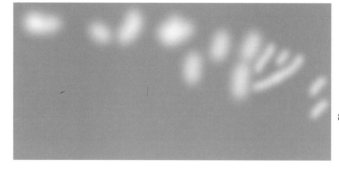

8 Using the Airbrush tool, I added small wisps of light tones to form the areas for displacement.

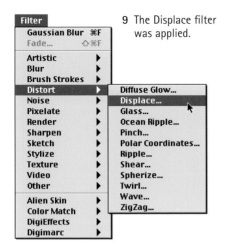

9 The Displace filter was applied.

10 In the Displace dialog box for the filter, I lowered the default setting to soften the effect.

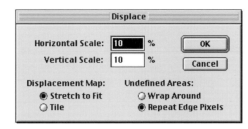

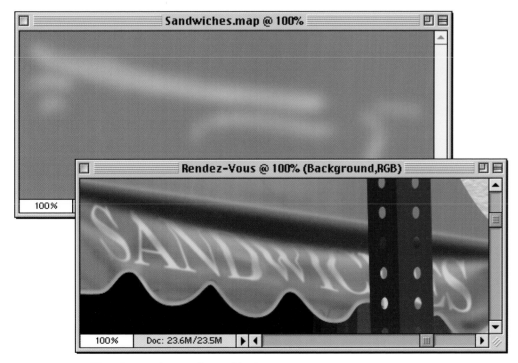

11 The result was text-bending, which gives the illusion of distortion by the folds in the awning fabric.

12 The other words were distorted in the same way.

file. It also makes me feel like such a power user.

n o t e | The Select>Save Selection procedure works best for large files. If you are working on small files such as Web images, then selecting all, copying, and pasting is fine.

The file for the displacement map was saved. I gave it a descriptive name and added the suffix **.map** to make it easy to find when the filter asked for it.

Then I deleted the alpha channel from the original document and deselected the selection I'd made for the transfer of the image data. The image was now in its original state, prior to the creation of the alpha channel, awaiting the distortion of the letters.

I then applied the Displace filter (Filter>Distort>Displace) and lowered the parameters from the default of 10 to soften the effect (Figures 9 and 10).

The text then bent to the values set in the displacement map, thus creating the effect of the letters following the folds on the awning (Figure 11).

I distorted the other words, using the same method (Figure 12). Then I created displacement maps for each.

In order to help you fully understand this extremely helpful feature, let's create something together. We are going to simulate the third dimension from a flat, 2D image. This will require bending the image.

Exercise 5.1   Stepping through an Open Book

To simulate the third dimension from a flat, 2D image, follow these steps:

1   Scan an opened magazine or book on a flatbed scanner (Figure 13).

2   Select the book and choose Layer>New Layer Via Cut to separate the book from the background and put it into its own layer (Figure 14).

3   Expand the canvas size to give you room to work in. Give it as much room as you see in Figure 14.

4   Using the Distort function (Edit> Transform>Distort), distort the book to give it an angled view—as if it were lying on a tabletop. Refer to Figure 15 for the angle you should attain.

5   Using the Polygonal Lasso tool or the Path tool, select the page on the right and create a new layer for it (Layer>New Layer Via Copy).

This will make a copy of the page and place it in its own layer, while leaving the original image below undisturbed (Figure 16).

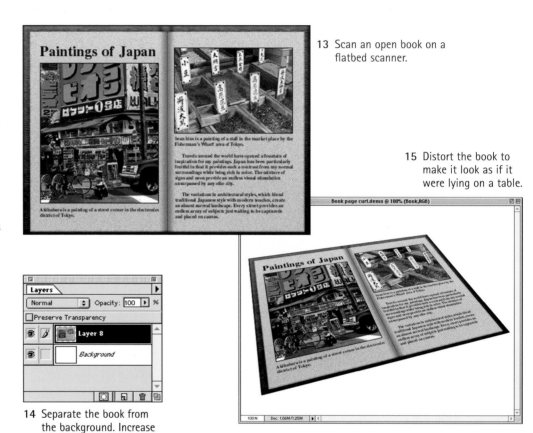

13 Scan an open book on a flatbed scanner.

15 Distort the book to make it look as if it were lying on a table.

14 Separate the book from the background. Increase the canvas size to give you room to work.

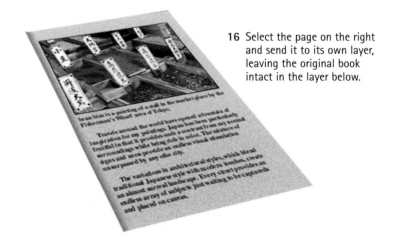

16 Select the page on the right and send it to its own layer, leaving the original book intact in the layer below.

Now it is time to create the displacement map used to bend the page.

6   Click on the Make New Channel icon at the bottom of the Channel palette to create a new alpha channel.

7   Make sure the eye icon is turned on for all the channels so that you can see the image through the alpha channel (Figure 17). The alpha channel will be selected as the channel to be written to, allowing you to create the map exactly where you want the effect to take place.

8   Using an Airbrush tool (large enough to create lines similar in size to the ones shown in Figures 18 and 19, and with white as the color), Shift-click to create two or three straight lines that form a thin cone.

    n o t e | Afterwards you might want to give the lines a Gaussian Blur filter to soften them.

9   When the channel is complete, select it all, copy the selection to the Clipboard, make a new document, paste the contents of the Clipboard into the new document, and flatten and save the new document with whatever name you choose.

    n o t e | If you are pasting the contents of the alpha channel into a new document, it falls into a layer of its own. This requires you to flatten the file.

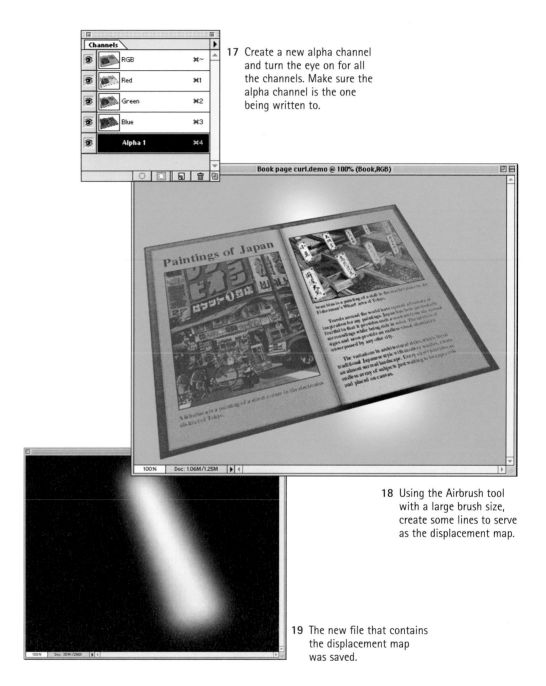

17 Create a new alpha channel and turn the eye on for all the channels. Make sure the alpha channel is the one being written to.

18 Using the Airbrush tool with a large brush size, create some lines to serve as the displacement map.

19 The new file that contains the displacement map was saved.

Exercise 5.1 Stepping through an Open Book *(continued)*

Or, as I did in my image, turn the channel into a selection with Select>Save Selection and save the selection to a new document. This method has fewer steps and happens instantly, bypassing the placing of large amounts of data into RAM. Whichever method you choose, make sure you save the document.

n o t e | The Save Selection procedure produces a file that has a single layer, so it does not require flattening.

10 Return to the file that contains the image of the book, make sure you have the layer with the individual page selected, and choose Filter>Distort>Displace, using the default settings.

11 When Photoshop asks you for the displacement map, use the one you created.

The result will be a page that looks curled (Figure 20). Cool, huh?

12 Move the page into position so that it looks right.

Because we have now created a third dimension, we must complete the effect by adding lights and shadows.

13 Create a new layer above the original book layer and below the curled page layer.

n o t e | When you create a new layer, Photoshop inserts the new layer directly above the currently selected layer.

14 Using the Airbrush tool and black, spray a soft shadow below the curled page; then, with the Eraser tool, eliminate any spills that might occur outside the edges of the page (Figure 21).

15 Create a new layer above the layer of the curled page to add highlights and shadows to the page.

16 Using the Airbrush tool in varying sizes, spray tones of black and white to represent highlights and shadows on the page, as shown in Figure 22.

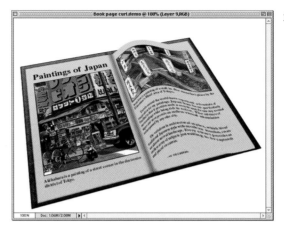

20 The filter creates a curling page.

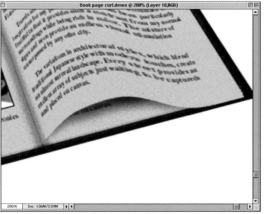

21 In a new layer, spray some black below the layer of the curled page to create a shadow caused by the upturned page.

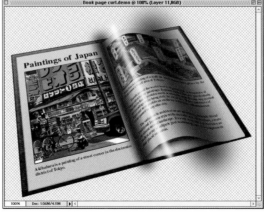

22 In yet another layer, create a series of black-and-white strokes to simulate the effect of light hitting the curled page.

17 Press the Option key (Alt on a PC) and click between the layer of the curled page and the highlight-and-shadow layer to create a *clipping group* (Figure 23).

This clipping group uses the transparent information of the lowest layer in the group as a mask for the layers in the group above it (Figure 24).

There you have it (Figure 25)! A way to bend things in Photoshop! Yep, it was always there.

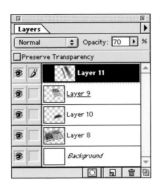

23 Turn the layer with the highlight and shadows into a clipping group with the layer of the curled page.

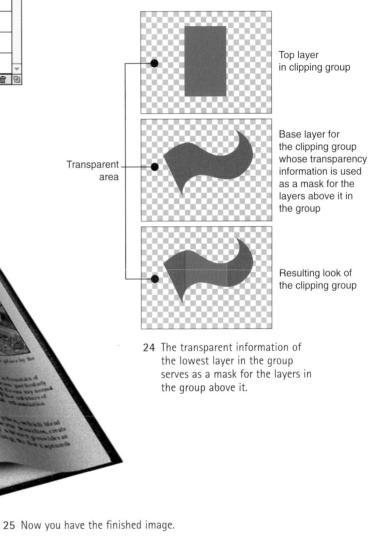

Top layer in clipping group

Transparent area

Base layer for the clipping group whose transparency information is used as a mask for the layers above it in the group

Resulting look of the clipping group

24 The transparent information of the lowest layer in the group serves as a mask for the layers in the group above it.

25 Now you have the finished image.

chapter 6

Creating a
Greener World

I was born on 139th Street in Manhattan, and I lived in New York City for 45 years. Trees were something I saw in books and on the occasional trip to Central Park. Paradoxically, I always loved to go camping and hiking in the woods.

In 1993, I moved to California. I now live in a redwood grove and see nothing but green as far as the eye can see. Do you think this change of scenery had an effect on my art? Well, before 1993, I painted old, dirty bars and storefronts. After 1993, I've painted old, not-so-dirty bars and storefronts, but they have a lot green around them.

The abundance and variety of foliage that surrounds me has become an interesting challenge for me to re-create. You might say that a bush is green, but, if you were to re-create it, you would have to use many different shades of green. A leaf has a specific shape, but leaves all grow in different directions. When you are trying to illustrate them, the leaves take on many shapes.

Through the years, I've developed many techniques for creating foliage. New features in programs such as Illustrator have given me new and more exciting techniques. In this chapter, we explore enough techniques to allow you to go out and play Johnny Appleseed—to create your own forest.

The images in Figure 1 focus on foliage, demonstrating a variety of techniques, not unlike some of the techniques I employed when I worked with brushes on canvas.

1 Two of these views can be seen in one of the focal images in this chapter. Can you guess which image?

2 The painting entitled *Miller* is a scene just down the street from my house.

Trees

Figure 2 shows the digital painting, *Miller*, my re-creation of a street behind my house. The scene in the painting is just down the street. I chose to render it in a color scheme that pays tribute to Maxfield Parrish, a great influence on my artistic career. This image is also the way I saw the scene one evening after the sun had gone down and night knocked on the door. As you can see, a variety of foliage is visible in the painting.

Unfortunately, I paint with light and have found it next to impossible to reproduce this image with the intensity of color with which it was created. If you want to view it in its actual colors, go to the New Riders Web site at www.newriders.com or to my site: www.crl.com/~bmonroy.

Where It All Begins

The first step was to create a sketch of the scene. Using Adobe Illustrator, I created an outline of the shapes that would make up the scene (Figure 3). All the paths were given a thin black stroke.

Normally, you would create these paths as closed paths that can be made into selections and filled with a color. But I wanted to use them simply as guides. I wanted to create the shapes of the trees with a sweeping motion of my hand, much as I would if I were using a traditional brush on canvas. Using the tools in Photoshop with my WACOM tablet allowed me to achieve that free-flowing motion.

After the shapes were complete, I copied them to the Clipboard and pasted them into a layer in Adobe Photoshop (Figure 4).

This layer, called "Outline," served as a guide for adding the color and details, in much the same way as traditional charcoal or pencil outlines are drawn on canvas to guide the application of paint.

A new layer was created in which the tree would be painted. Using the Paintbrush tool with a color chosen for the tree in the foreground, I painted the outline (Figure 5).

The filter I used was Add Noise (Filter>Noise>Add Noise), which comes with Photoshop. I set the filter to Monochrome mode, which gave me random noise made from variations of the existing color. This became the starting point for the texture of the tree's bark (Figure 6).

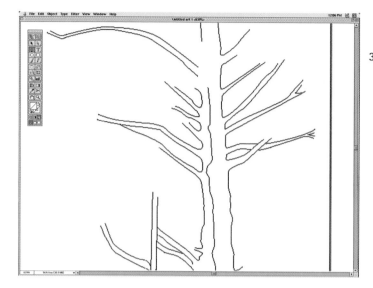

3 In Illustrator, I created the shapes to outline the overall scene.

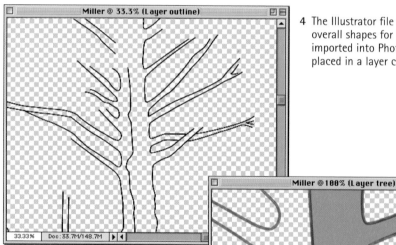

4 The Illustrator file with the overall shapes for the image was imported into Photoshop and placed in a layer called "Outline."

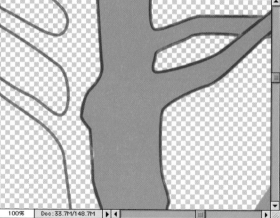

5 Using the Outline layer as a guide, the shape of the tree was painted by using the Paintbrush tool and a treelike color.

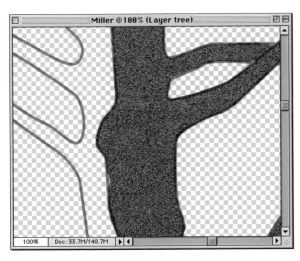

6 I applied the Add Noise filter to get a strong contrasting noise, which served as the basis for the texture of the tree's bark.

Next, I applied another filter to get the rough bark effect. I chose Mosaic Tiles (Filter>Texture>Mosaic Tiles), as shown in Figure 7. This achieved the desired effect for the texture of the tree (Figure 8).

Making sure that Preserve Transparency was selected, and using the Airbrush tool with brushes of various sizes, shadows were added to the tree and lines cut into the back, thus adding detail to the texture (Figure 9).

7 The Mosaic Tiles filter was applied to complete the bark texture for the tree.

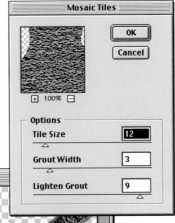

The Preserve Transparency option ensures that any modification to a layer will apply only to the pixels that make up the image within the layer and will not affect the transparent portion of the layer.

In another new layer, the same technique was used on the second tree visible in back; a slightly different color separates the two.

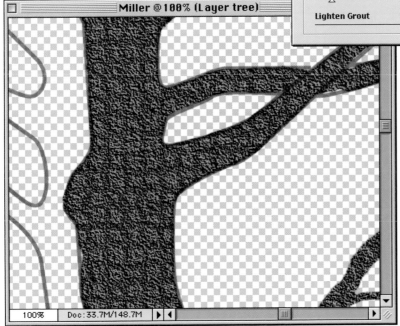

8 This final filter completed the bark texture for the tree.

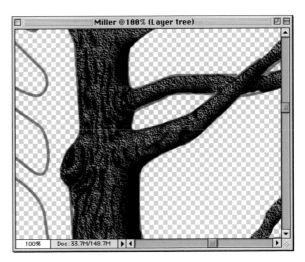

9 Using the Airbrush tool, various grooves were painted onto the bark of the tree.

117

What Comes Next

Now came the challenge of creating the leaves.

Watch some early Bob Smith shows on TV while he creates one of his beautiful landscapes. He creates leaves on trees, bushes, or fields of blossoms by continuously dabbing the canvas with a brush full of paint of the appropriate color. The technique you are about to learn uses this identical method.

One great advantage is that your brush can be specialized. Photoshop gives you the ability to select any part of an image and convert it into a custom brush.

In a new file, I created a series of shapes to form leaf clusters. Using the Paintbrush tool, with black for my color, I created little clusters of different leaves (Figure 10). In some cases, I simply flipped or rotated some of the clusters I had already created to form additional clusters.

After individually selecting these different shapes with the Rectangle selection tool, I turned them into brush shapes (Figure 11) by choosing Define Brush from the Brushes palette's drop-down menu.

The same technique was used to create many different shapes to be used for the other trees and the bushes in front (Figure 12).

With the Paintbrush tool and the various leaf cluster-shaped brushes, the leaves were added to the trees.

First, using black, I created a layer of leaves that would serve not only as the overall shape, but also as the leaves in the shadow areas behind the tree (Figure 13). These leaves were blocked from the light by the leaves in the foreground, and they were too far from the light source to be illuminated.

Like the traditional technique utilized in the brush-on-canvas method, the Paintbrush tool was continuously clicked over the area to create many leaves. This was a click action, with no drag of the mouse. Dragging the mouse would cause the brush to smear the leaf shapes into lines.

I switched brush shapes on occasion to create the appearance of random leaves.

In another layer, using various shades of orange and different Opacity settings for the brush, additional leaves were created (Figure 14). These leaves are in front and seem to be catching the light.

The same technique was then used to create the bushes and all the other trees visible throughout the image.

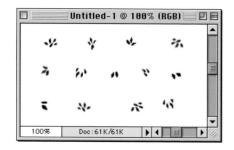

10 Using the Paintbrush tool, various clusters of leaves were created.

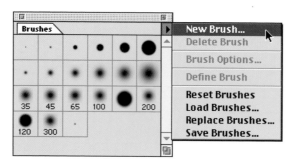

11 The leaf clusters were individually selected and defined as brushes in the Brushes palette.

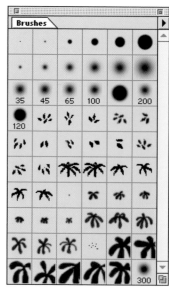

12 This Brushes palette contains many of the shapes I used to create foliage.

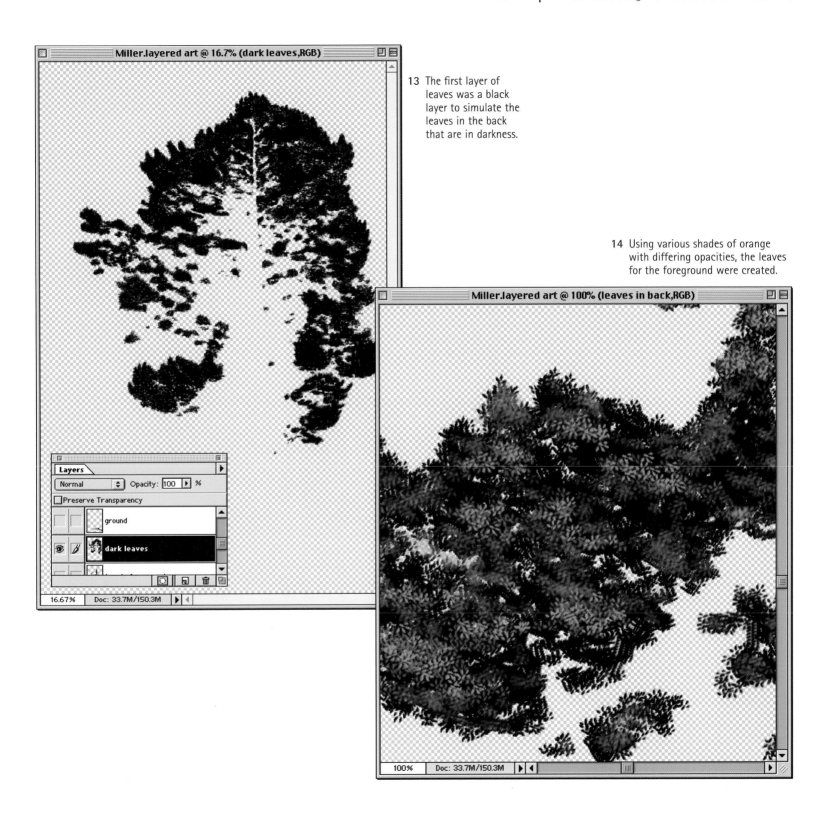

13 The first layer of leaves was a black layer to simulate the leaves in the back that are in darkness.

14 Using various shades of orange with differing opacities, the leaves for the foreground were created.

More on Trees

The *Cedar* image has foliage all over the place, including a couple of trees on either side of the scene (Figure 15). The foliage for this painting had to be created with much more detail than that in the *Miller* image because you are much closer to the subject here than you are in the *Miller* image,

Being this close to the trees and bushes also requires more accuracy in the depiction of the shapes of the foliage.

15 The *Cedar* image has all kinds of foliage—bushes, trees, and weeds. Weeds—what would any area of green be without them?

© Bert Monroy 1996

120

A Closer Look at Bark

The bark for these trees and those in the *Miller* image were created in the same way, except for the filters used.

The trees in Figure 16 are closer to the foreground and more exposed, so they required far more detail.

I started by creating the basic shape of the tree in its own layer and then applied the Add Noise (Filter>Noise>Add Noise) to the shape. As with the tree barks in *Miller*, Monochrome was selected for the filter to avoid the introduction of any unwanted colors.

Next, I used the Craquelure filter (Filter> Texture>Craquelure) to complete the basic bark texture (Figure 17). This texture was closer to the actual tree bark and gave me a better basis from which to build my trees.

I added texture with the Paintbrush tool by using the small round shapes in the same fashion as in the *Miller* trees, and by painting grooves in the bark.

By selecting certain areas, filling them with an appropriate color, and adding noise, I created portions of the bark that had been damaged over time (Figure 18).

16 These trees are much closer
to the viewer, so they
required more detail than
the ones in *Miller*.

17 The Craquelure filter
finalized the basic
bark texture.

18 I created the appearance
of damaged bark.

A Closer Look at Leaves

The leaves were created in much the same way as they were in *Miller*, although these leaves required some additional attention to detail.

The various shapes for the leaves were created and used as brush shapes (Figure 19). In this case, the shapes were individual leaves rather than clusters of leaves. Once again, variety was achieved by making duplicates of shapes, and flipping and rotating them to form additional leaf shapes.

Using varying shades of green, I clicked the brush shapes in their own layer to form the foliage on the tree. I used multiple layers to create a diversity of color (Figure 20). The darker leaves and those hidden from the light were placed in layers in back. Lighter-colored leaves were placed in additional layers.

Different layers were assigned different modes, and that gave the illusion of shadows cast on some leaves by other leaves. (Changing the mode for a layer affects the way it relates to layers below it.) By experimenting with these different modes, I was able to achieve a great range of leaf colors and effects.

Using the Dodge and Burn tools, additional touches were added to individual leaves (Figure 21). In some cases, the Paintbrush tool was used to add a dab of color to a leaf in order to give the leaf some texture and dimension.

19 To create the leaves, I again made shapes and defined them as brushes.

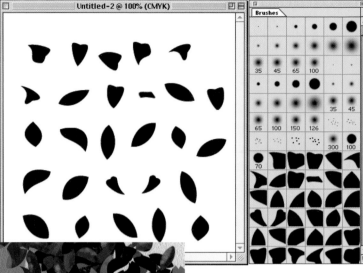

20 Multiple layers of leaves, in different modes, were used to add diversity.

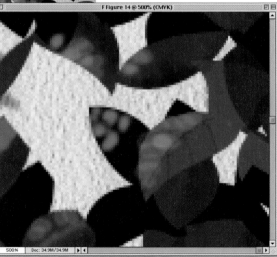

21 Additional dimension and texture were given to individual leaves.

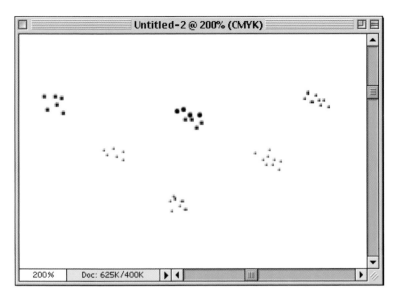

22 Clusters of dots served as the basis for the grass custom brushes.

23 The Brush Options dialog box allows you to set the amount of space between the shape of the brush that is applied to the canvas as the tool is dragged along.

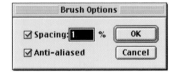

24 Use the Fade value to simulate effects of a paintbrush.

25 The grassy areas in both *Miller* and *Cedar* were created with the Paintbrush tool and custom brushes set to fade out.

Other Greenery

Now that you've got a handle on creating trees, you're probably ready to take on other green stuff. Just look around you; the world is a lot greener than you might realize!

The Grass Is Greener

The grass visible at the ground level of both the *Miller* and *Cedar* images was created with a variation of the technique used for the leaves on the trees. For the grass, I created a cluster of dots to serve as the basis for the brush shape (Figure 22). As with the leaves, different clusters were created to avoid the similarity in shape that a viewer would be sure to spot. Grass, like leaves, must appear to be totally random in nature.

When a custom brush is created, the spacing for it is set to 25% by default. This means that as you apply a stroke with a designated shape, it is spaced so that it can be seen as a distinct shape.

In the case of the leaves and leaf clusters, this spacing was irrelevant because they were applied as individual clicks with the Paintbrush tool rather than with the click-and-drag method.

The grass is a different story. In this case, the Paintbrush tool is dragged along to form the foliage.

Double-clicking on the brush shape in the Brushes palette pops up the Brush Options dialog box (Figure 23). Here, I entered the value of 1%, the lowest value accepted. This ensured that the stroke would be a continuous application of color.

I set a Fade value for the Paintbrush tool (Figure 24) to simulate the effect of a paintbrush running out of paint or being lifted gradually from the surface of the canvas.

Using multiple brush shapes and shades of color for variety, the grassy areas were created (Figure 25).

One Good Leaf Leads
to Another

The other foliage throughout required specific labor for its creation. Notice the bush to the left of the doorway in the *Cedar* image (Figure 26). This is a specific type of plant. If I hadn't created it as it really is, I am sure I would get e-mail from scores of horticulturists wanting to educate me on the proper look of the plant. Don't laugh; it has happened.

I took an actual leaf from the site to use as reference. It had fallen off and was lying on the ground. (Don't think I go around picking leaves off of other people's plants.)

In Illustrator, I created three or four basic shapes for the leaves (Figure 27) and then distorted, flipped, and rotated these shapes to make additional leaves. I also filled the shapes with different shades of green to add more distinction between the leaves.

The leaves were imported into the Photoshop file as pixels (Figure 28). Because I added the color in Illustrator, it wasn't necessary to import the paths.

As the leaves were imported, I placed them into clusters to resemble the way the leaves were growing on the bush. I created each cluster in its own layer to make further modification easier (Figure 29).

26 In the *Cedar* image, a bush with large leaves is next to the door.

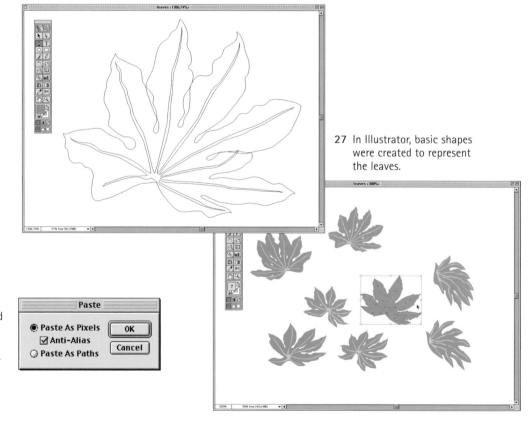

27 In Illustrator, basic shapes were created to represent the leaves.

28 The leaves were imported into Photoshop as pixels because the color had been added in Illustrator.

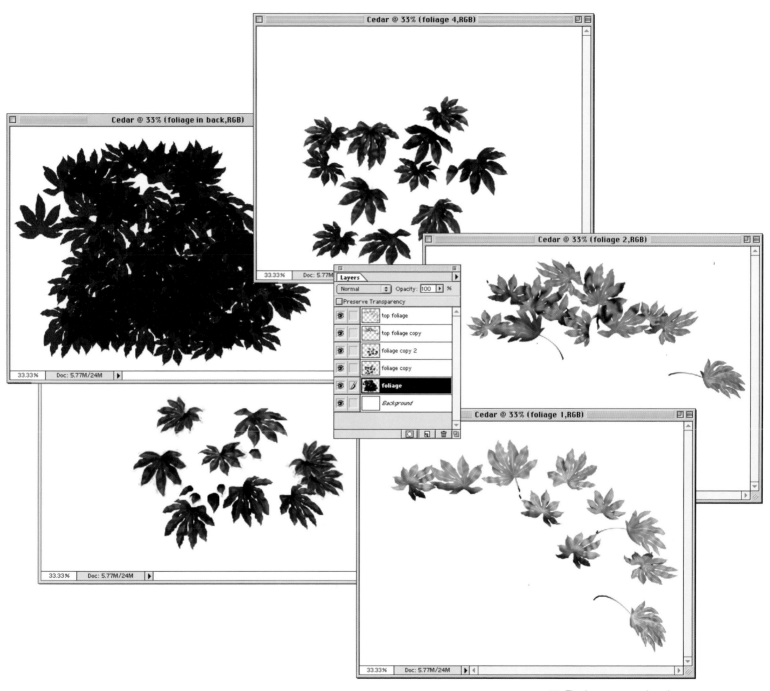

29 The leaves were placed as clusters into multiple layers.

I adjusted the color and saturation in different layers to simulate depth. The layer farthest back was filled with black, giving it the look of leaves on which the light is completely blocked by the leaves in front. Using the Dodge and Burn tools, I added shadows and highlights to selected leaves (Figure 30). Wherever one leaf overlapped another, I made sure to create a shadow on the lower leaf to give it that sense of spatial relationship.

Some leaves were further distorted and colored with browns to simulate leaves that have fallen off the bush (Figure 31). (It was one of these, by the way, that I took for reference.)

Even the Weeds Look Good

The weeds you see throughout the foreground were created the same way. Those in the foreground of the images, shown in Figure 32, were all created in Illustrator and imported into Photoshop, where highlights and shadow were added.

30 Shading and highlights were added with the Dodge and Burn tools to give the leaves dimensionality.

31 Some leaves were further distorted and colored with warm tones to simulate leaves that had fallen off the bush.

32 What exterminator would have the heart to kill these beautiful weeds?

Laurel Leaves Come from Distortion

A focal image in the chapter "Working with Wood and Metal" is
the gate, shown in Figure 33. Figure 34 is a close-up of the leaves
of the laurel at the side of the gate. These leaves were created in
Illustrator from a single leaf that was distorted. The color was also
modified from leaf to leaf to add diversity (Figure 35). The realistic
texture and shading you see in Figure 36 were added in Photoshop.

33 *the gate.*

© Bert Monroy 1997

34 The image *the gate* has a laurel bush treatments at the side of the gate.

35 The leaves were created by importing shapes from Illustrator into Photoshop.

36 The realistic details on the leaves were added in Photoshop.

Redwood Branches Begin with a Twig and a Needle

The branches of the redwood trees in *the gate* were also created in Illustrator. A single branch was made from a single twig and one needle (Figure 37). The needle was replicated several times and placed along the edges of the twig, adjusting the angle and color, ever so slightly to avoid similarity (Figure 38).

The branches were constructed in many configurations and imported into Photoshop where they were placed in position over the gate. Figure 39 shows a close-up of the branches.

37 The redwood branches were made from a single twig and needle.

38 By changing the original redwood branch, I created many branches.

39 The branches were imported into
Photoshop and placed over the gate.

the gate @ 100% (Background,RGB)

100%   Doc: 29.4M/28.2M

Scatter Brush:
A New Path to a Greener World

To create the image called *The Raven*, shown in Figure 40, I used a new technique that became available with Illustrator 8. The tree on the right came from the new Scatter brush feature, which you'll learn about if you keep on reading.

40 In the image *The Raven*, I employed a new feature introduced in Illustrator 8.

In Illustrator, I created a series of leaves that contained as much detail as I felt would be distinguishable after the leaves were imported into Photoshop. (I could add tons of detail, but the leaves would appear quite small in the Photoshop file. When the leaves come into Photoshop, they get rasterized to the resolution of the Photoshop file. Detail gets broken up into pixels.) With this in mind, I gave the leaves color and just enough detail to give them the semblance of real leaves.

n o t e | The resolution and size of the file you work on will determine how much detail will be carried over from Illustrator to Photoshop. The image I am showing here was set to 350dpi, with a dimension of 11 inches by 8 inches. The leaves measure a mere quarter of an inch, which limited the amount of detail I could give them.

The leaves were made with various colors; to complete the detail, they had veins, shadows, and highlights (Figure 41). I arranged the leaves into a small cluster and selected them all.

41 Leaves were created with as much detail as I felt would carry over into Photoshop after they were rasterized and reduced.

I chose New Brush from the drop-down menu of the Brushes palette (Figure 42). When you select a new brush, a dialog box pops up in which you can choose the type of brush you are creating (Figure 43). I made mine a Scatter Brush. After that selection is made, another dialog box appears in which attributes can be assigned to the brush.

The Scatter Brush would distribute the brush shape along any path I created. I wanted the paths to serve as branches, with the leaves growing out from them.

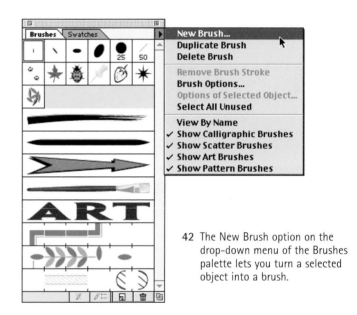

42 The New Brush option on the drop-down menu of the Brushes palette lets you turn a selected object into a brush.

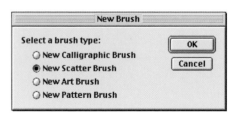

43 When you choose to make a new brush, you can choose the type of brush you will create.

I wanted the leaves to appear as random as possible throughout the limbs of the tree, so I chose Random for all the attributes (Figure 44). The Random option lets you set parameters by which the brush will create its stroke.

I chose the following settings:

- I set the Size to randomize within a small percentage (68–100%) because I didn't want leaves to be too small or too large. I wanted some uniformity to the size. The higher the size percentage differential, the more extreme the variety of sizes between the leaves being generated. A large difference would have made the branches look as if they contained different-sized leaves, which would not be the case. I just wanted a slight change in size to simulate distance from the viewer.

- Spacing sets the distance between the brush shapes; in this case, the clusters of leaves. I wanted them to be close together, as they would appear on a real tree.

- Scatter distributes the brush shape on either side of the path that is being stroked with the custom brush. I wanted the leaf clusters to stay within the path, so I set these parameters very low.

- Rotation was also set to small parameters so that the leaves would appear to be facing in a similar direction, pointing up toward the sun.

With the brush completed, I set out to build the branches for my tree (Figure 45). I set the branches as clusters that would be imported individually into Photoshop.

Each of these branches was given its own layer in which could be further modified (Figure 46). Like the previous examples, these individual layers would be modified to resemble darker branches hidden from the light.

After all the layers were in place, they were merged into a single layer. This layer was duplicated and filled with black, to serve as the shadow of the tree on the building behind it (Figure 47). The layer for the shadow was scaled down in size because the shadow is farther from the tree. I also blurred the shadow slightly by using the Gaussian Blur filter to soften the edges.

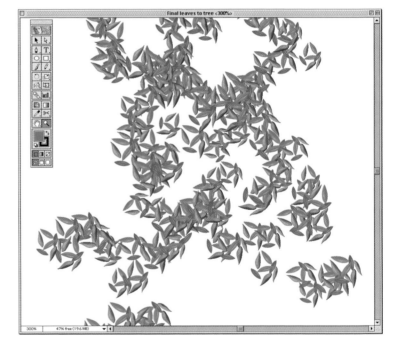

45 To form branches of the tree, I created and stroked Paths with the leaf-cluster Scatter Brush.

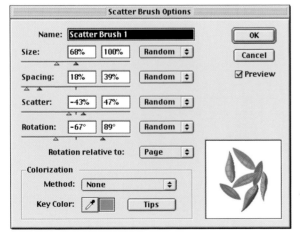

44 In the Scatter Brush Options dialog box, you can set a multitude of parameters for the brush.

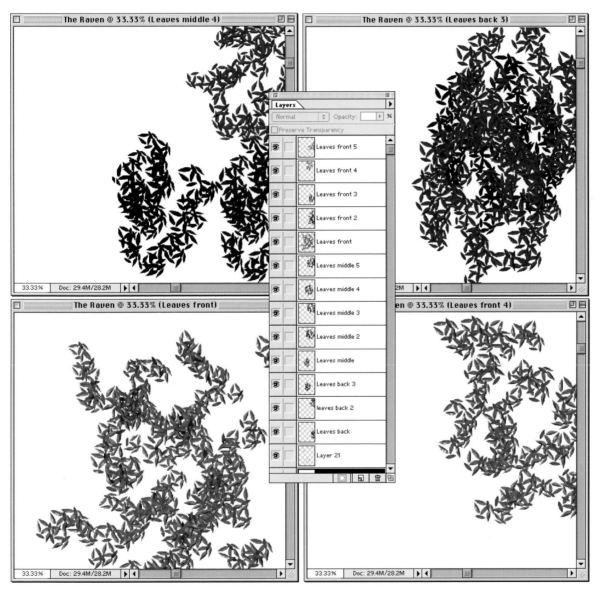

46 The branches were imported into Photoshop, where they were assigned their own layers.

47 The layer of the tree served as the basis for the shadow of the tree on the scene behind it.

Recycled Greenery

In the course of creating all these effects, I always keep various versions of an image because I find it advantageous to give elements different purposes for other situations. The tree you just saw in the image *The Raven* can be seen in other paintings as well.

For example, the tree in *The Raven* served to create the tree shadow as well as the plants in the planters outside the *Rendezvous* in Figure 48. It also became the tree down the street for *The Studio theater* (Figure 49).

48 The tree from *The Raven* can be seen as bushes in the planters of the *Rendez-vous.*

© Bert Monroy 1999

A closer look at the images at the beginning of this chapter will reveal that both images on the left in Figure 1 show trees created in the *Miller* image.

49 The tree from *The Raven* is also the tree down the street in *The Studio Theater*.

chapter 7

Working with Wood and Metal

Now that we have gone through all the criteria for building the elements of an image, the only thing left is to give those elements an actual material. You can create a ball, but what it is made of will give it its final identity within the context of the overall image. The material also adds realism to an object by giving the viewer a point of reference by which to establish that reality.

A wooden table without a wood grain will appear to be made of plastic. If you were doing a portrait of a person, the skin would not be gray and highly reflective—unless your aim was to make the person seem to be made of metal. Therefore, all objects should be given the characteristics of the material they are made of.

Many companies sell textures that can be incorporated into your illustration. They provide you with every wood and stone texture known to man. You might even find a few you didn't know existed. Textiles, sands, you name it—they've got 'em.

You also have the option of scanning textures from real-life materials. I was once working on an illustration for an ad agency, and I needed a wooden texture for a large wooden door in the illustration—fast. The speakers from my stereo system were made of a nice oak, exactly what I was looking for. I took one of the speakers, placed it right on top of my scanner, and scanned in the texture. Voilá! All I had to do at that point was distort the flat texture to the shape of the door in the illustration, and I was done.

These textures can also be used as texture maps for creating 3D elements in a 3D program. In this chapter, however, we will go through the process of creating textures from scratch.

Photoshop comes with a vast array of filters that, used creatively, can be very effective for generating just about any texture you need. We will also explore the using of some additional Illustrator and Photoshop techniques for creating realistic textures.

1 The *marble and matches* image has a few wooden matches.

Beginning with Wood

Let's start with one of the most common materials found in our everyday life: wood. Look around you and you will see many items made of wood. Wood, however, is not just wood. There is oak, pine, mahogany, and so on. It is polished, weathered, rough, smooth—the list goes on and on.

Some woods have very specific patterns to their texture, but most woods have similar grains. The major difference is usually the color. You can create the look of different woods by simply using the methods in this chapter and choosing a color to match the wood you are trying to emulate.

The wood's look and feel will be strongly influenced by where you use it. Let's look at a very simple wooden texture. By *simple,* I mean a texture without knots or other distinguishing characteristics.

An Image of Marble and Matches

The *marble and matches* image has a few wooden matches hanging around, minding their own business (Figure 1). Granted, they are black, but they're obviously made of wood. They are colored black just to make them look cool, but let's face it—a wood of any other color is still wood.

The shapes, which in this case are simple rectangles, were created with the Path tool in Photoshop (Figure 2).

2 The shapes for the matchsticks were created with the Path tool.

In a new layer, the paths were made into selections and filled with a medium gray tone (Figure 3). Each side of a matchstick was generated individually in its own layer. This was necessary to get all the wood grains to follow the different directions of each stick.

I then selected the Add Noise filter. I added a large quantity of noise to the shape (Figure 4).

The Motion Blur filter was then employed to complete the texture (Figure 5). The angle for the filter was set to match the angle of the matchsticks. The distance was set long enough to give the grain enough length. Finally, the Dodge and Burn tools were used to add dark areas and highlights to the matchsticks.

As mentioned before, this procedure was used for each individual stick. They could not all be done at the same time because each matchstick was placed in a different direction.

This process can be effective for creating most wooden textures. Slight variations can be employed for other situations.

3 The paths were made into selections and filled with a medium gray tone.

4 The Add Noise filter was used to add a large quantity of noise to the shape of the matchstick.

5 The Motion Blur filter added the effect of the wood grain, with its direction set to follow that of the matchstick.

A Handle of Wood

I was commissioned by an ad agency to create a scene of a construction site (Figure 6). The scene was to include various pieces of heavy equipment, miscellaneous other items, and a man standing in the rain, taking notes. In the illustration, a hand shovel was to be visible just to the left of the man. To create the wooden sections of the shovel, I used the same procedure introduced in the preceding section, but with a slight variation (Figure 7).

6 This construction site illustration was commissioned by an ad agency for a client's brochure.

As with the matches, the shovel was created with the Path tool. The wood in this case was not colored, but was to have the natural brown hues that one would find on a shovel of this type. Because the handle and stem were to run in different directions, each was created separately.

I turned the path for the handle into a selection and created a new layer to house the handle (Figure 8). Then I filled the selection with a medium-brown color.

At this point, the process for creating the shovel differs from that used with the matchsticks. With the selection still active, I created another layer and then expanded the selection, using the Expand command (Select>Modify>Expand), as shown in Figure 9. Expanding a selection is limited to 16 pixels. I needed an area larger than this, so I expanded the selection three times, which gave me a selected area expanded by 48 pixels.

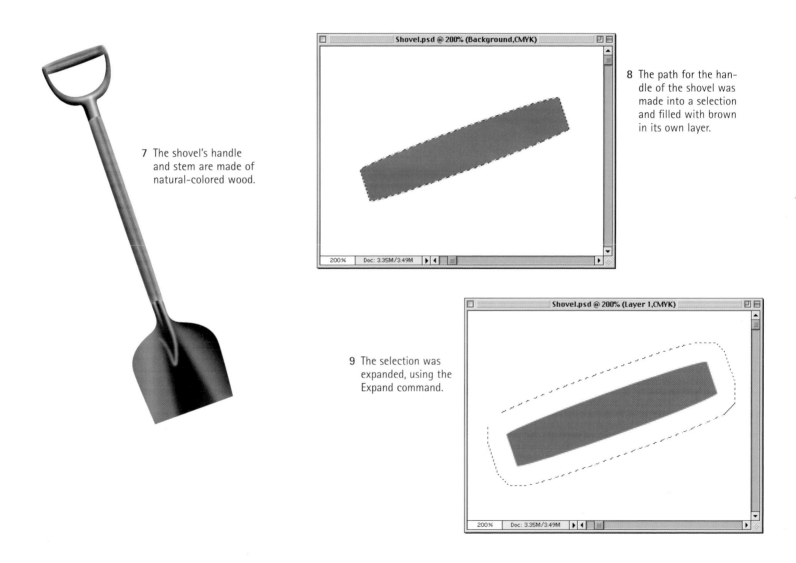

7 The shovel's handle and stem are made of natural-colored wood.

8 The path for the handle of the shovel was made into a selection and filled with brown in its own layer.

9 The selection was expanded, using the Expand command.

143

In this new layer, the expanded selection was again filled with brown. The Add Noise filter was applied to add the noise for the basis of the wood grain.

I lowered the layer's opacity so that I could see the layer that contained the shape of the handle (Figure 10). This would make it easy to set the angle in the Motion Blur filter to follow the angle for the handle.

I expanded the selection because the Motion Blur filter tends to use colors from outside the edges of a selected area (Figure 11). Although this was acceptable in the case of the matchstick because the match was colored black, any intrusion from the transparent area of the handle's layer would appear as light-gray areas in the wood. This would not be acceptable for the shovel's natural-colored wooden handle.

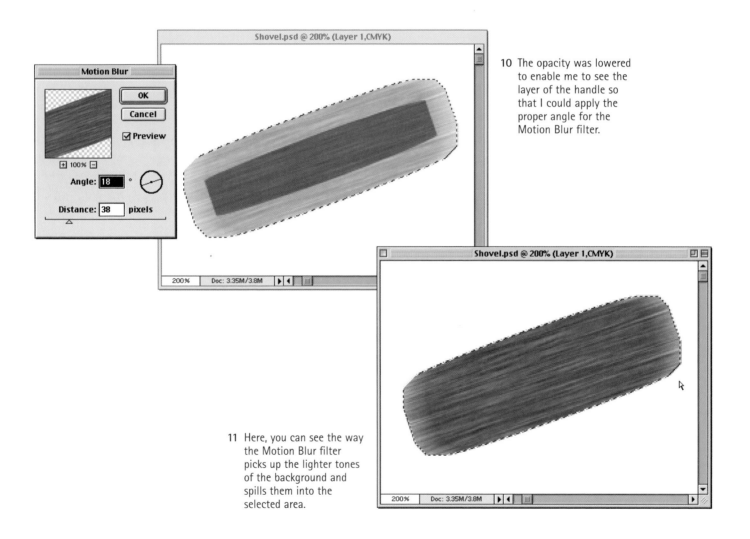

10 The opacity was lowered to enable me to see the layer of the handle so that I could apply the proper angle for the Motion Blur filter.

11 Here, you can see the way the Motion Blur filter picks up the lighter tones of the background and spills them into the selected area.

After the grain texture was complete, the layer of the handle and the layer of the grain were turned into a clipping group and then merged into a single layer.

Because the size of the handle is much larger than that of the tiny matchsticks, it will react to light in a much more apparent fashion. It is also necessary to establish the fact that the handle is rounded, not flat. Remember shadows? They add dimension.

Using the Dodge and Burn tools, I added highlights and shadows to simulate the effect of light hitting the handle (Figure 12).

Adding grit to the shovel was the final touch of realism. A shovel at a construction site does not stay clean very long. Even Felix Unger wouldn't be able to keep it clean. Obviously, this shovel has been used because it is sticking out of a pile of dirt.

Using the Clone tool with its opacity reduced, I cloned bits of the dirt on the ground onto the shapes of the shovel (Figure 13). The reason I reduced the opacity was to pick up just enough tonality to simulate a dirty shovel rather than a shovel caked with dirt. By varying the amount of opacity, I was able to show different amounts of dirt on different parts of the shovel.

Let's try a simple exercise together and create some wood.

12 Highlight and shadows were added to the handle to give it dimension.

13 Dirt from the ground was cloned over the shovel to give it that dirty look.

145

Exercise 7.1   Stepping through Wood

To create some wood, follow these steps:

1   In a new Photoshop document, click the Make New Layer icon at the bottom of the Layers palette to create a new layer.

2   In the new layer, create the shape you want to fill with the wood grain and then fill the shape with a brown color for the wood (Figure 14).

3   Create another layer and fill the entire layer with the same brown. Choose Filter>Noise> Add Noise. Make sure Monochromatic is selected and choose a substantial amount of noise to give you a coarse grain, as shown in Figure 15.

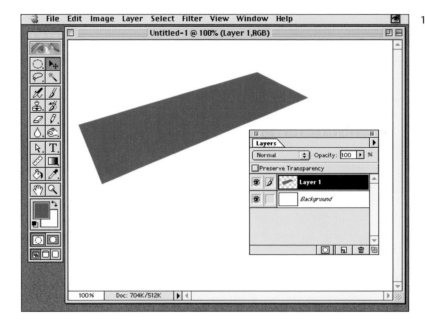

14   In a layer, select a shape and fill it with brown.

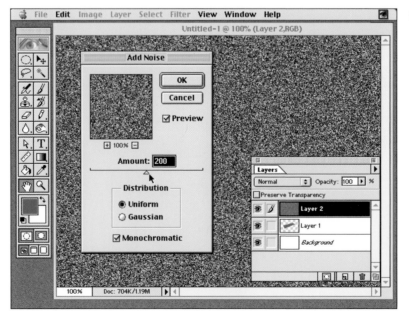

15   Create a new layer and fill it with the same brown color.

4 On the layer with the noise, lower the opacity just enough to see the wood shape in the layer below it. Choose the Motion Blur filter (Filter>Blur>Motion Blur). Select an angle to match the direction you want the wood grain to follow on the wood plank. Choose the amount of Motion Blur to give you the length of grain you want (Figure 16).

5 Bring the opacity back to 100%. Now merge the two layers into one by clicking between the two layers in the Layers palette while you press the Option (Alt on a PC) key.

6 Using both the Dodge and Burn tools with varying brush sizes, lighten and darken portions of the wooden shape to add additional grain texture, as in Figure 17.

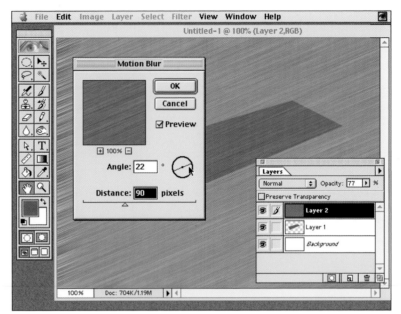

16 Lower the opacity to make the layer with the shape visible and apply the Motion Blur filter with an angle that matches the angle of the shape below.

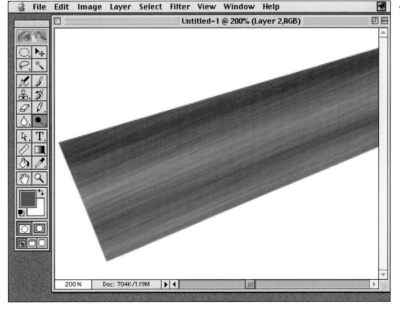

17 With the Dodge and Burn tools, add areas of shadow and highlight.

A Walk through a Gate

The process I have just outlined was simple enough for the particular elements contained in the images shown. The image entitled *the gate* required a little more time and effort (Figure 18).

Notice that this time the wood grain does have certain characteristics that make each plank of the gate unique (Figure 19). The planks have knots that intrude on the smoothness of the grain. The grain itself follows different directions and shapes within the visible area of the wood.

© Bert Monroy 1997

18 *the gate.*

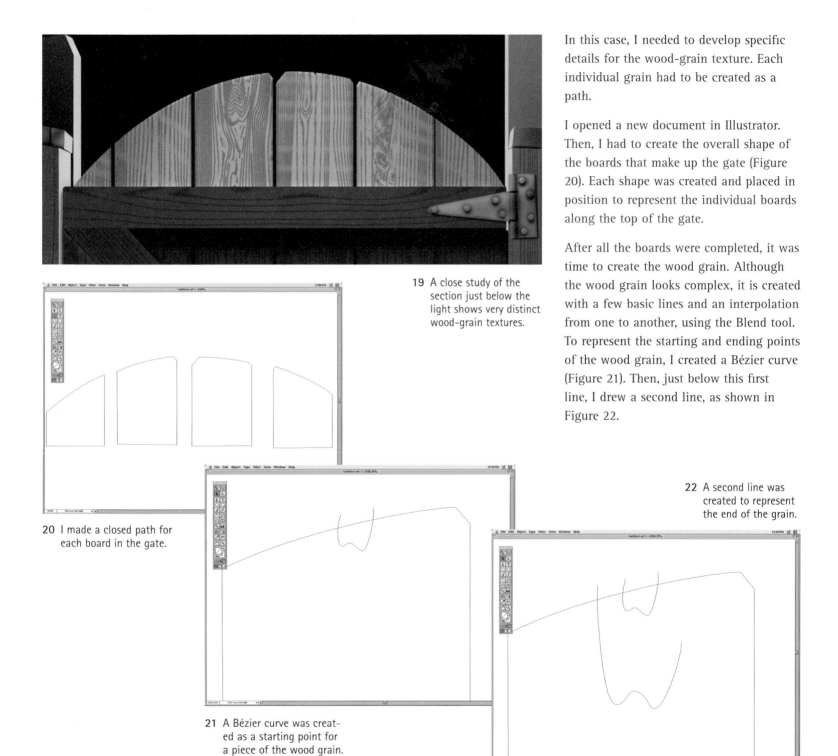

In this case, I needed to develop specific details for the wood-grain texture. Each individual grain had to be created as a path.

I opened a new document in Illustrator. Then, I had to create the overall shape of the boards that make up the gate (Figure 20). Each shape was created and placed in position to represent the individual boards along the top of the gate.

After all the boards were completed, it was time to create the wood grain. Although the wood grain looks complex, it is created with a few basic lines and an interpolation from one to another, using the Blend tool. To represent the starting and ending points of the wood grain, I created a Bézier curve (Figure 21). Then, just below this first line, I drew a second line, as shown in Figure 22.

19 A close study of the section just below the light shows very distinct wood-grain textures.

20 I made a closed path for each board in the gate.

22 A second line was created to represent the end of the grain.

21 A Bézier curve was created as a starting point for a piece of the wood grain.

149

The Blend tool went through a change in Illustrator 8. To determine the way the tool will function, you now double-click on the tool in the Toolbox. A dialog box will appear when you do. In the dialog box, I chose Specified Steps as the Spacing and 6 as the number of steps the Blend tool would make (Figure 23).

Having selected both lines and using the Blend tool, I clicked on one of the end points of the first line and then on the same point of the other line. Six new lines appeared that blended in shape from one path to the other. Illustrator creates these blends as complete objects. I needed them to be individual paths, so I chose the Expand feature from the Object menu. This turned the six new lines into six independent paths.

Because these paths would be stroked in Photoshop with a color to represent the grain in the wood, it was crucial to space them adequately so that the final effect would not have them blend into each other.

To complete the remaining grains, I used a variety of vertical lines and curves and the same technique (Figure 24).

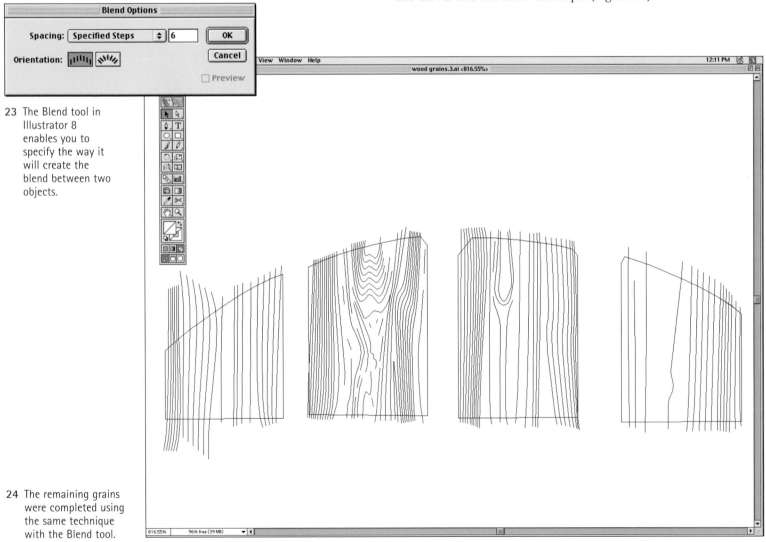

23 The Blend tool in Illustrator 8 enables you to specify the way it will create the blend between two objects.

24 The remaining grains were completed using the same technique with the Blend tool.

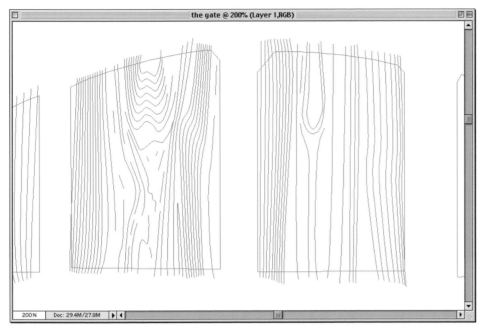

When all the paths needed to complete the wood grain for the top portion of the gate had been created, I imported them into Photoshop as paths, via the Clipboard, and placed them in position over the area for the top portion of the gate (Figure 25). A new layer was created to hold the grain.

The imported paths fell into the Paths palette as a Work Path. I immediately saved them by dragging them over the Save Path icon (Document icon) at the bottom of the Paths palette, and I named the Work Path "all paths" (Figure 26).

All the paths were imported as a whole, but it was necessary to separate the paths for the wooden boards from the paths for the grains. I duplicated the path by dragging it over the Save Path icon at the bottom of the Paths palette, selected and deleted the paths for the grain, and then renamed the path "boards" (Figure 27).

25 The paths were imported into Photoshop and placed in position for the top of the gate.

26 The path was named "all paths" to make it easy to identify after additional paths were created.

27 The path was duplicated. All the paths for the grain were deleted, and the resulting path was named "boards."

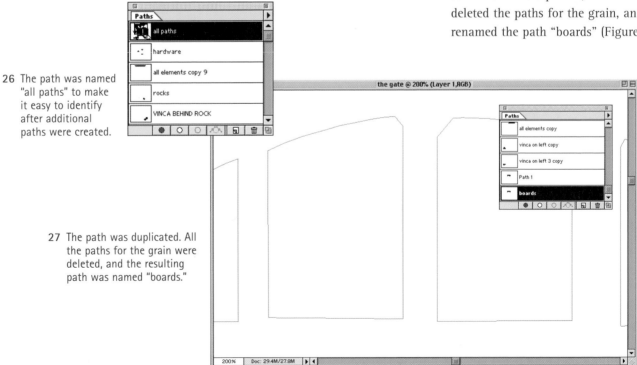

The path "all paths" was duplicated again. This time I deleted the paths for the boards, leaving behind the paths that would eventually be used to render the wood grain. This new path was named "grain" (Figure 28).

Now it was time to render the gate.

After creating a new layer to house the elements of the gate, I made the path "boards" a selection and then, using a series of brown tones, filled the shapes. The top portion of the boards was filled with a lighter gradient (Figure 29) to duplicate the effect of light spilling down over the gate from the hanging lantern. The area below the crossbeam would be hidden from the light, so it would be much darker than the rest of the gate.

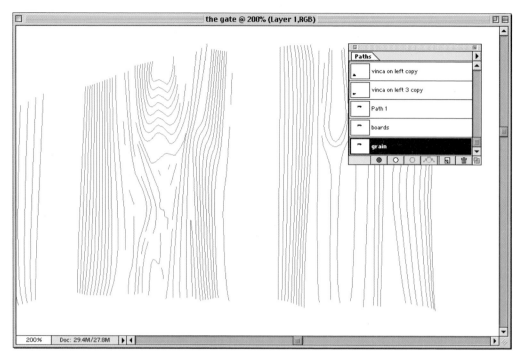

28 The paths for the wood grains were put into their own "grain" path in the palette.

I created another layer to contain the actual wood grain. The path for the grain was made active so that it could be seen over the boards. I selected the Airbrush tool; then, in the Brushes palette, I chose a size that would be thick enough to be seen but not so thick that neighboring grains would bleed into each other, filling in the area and becoming a thick mass. I then chose a color for the grain. Because the Airbrush tool was selected, simply dragging the path over the Stroke Path icon at the bottom of the Paths palette stroked the path (Figure 30).

> **n o t e** | When you use the Stroke Path option icon on the bottom of the Path palette and you are currently using the Path tool, the resulting stroke uses the Pencil tool to stroke the path as a default. If you have another tool selected, the Stroke Path function will use the currently selected tool to stroke the path.

Because the grain was in its own layer, it was easy to adjust the opacity until the desired tonality was achieved.

29 The path for the boards at the top of the gate was made into a selection and filled with a wood hue gradient.

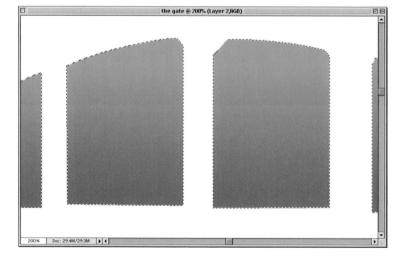

30 The path containing all the individual paths for the wood grain was stroked, using the Airbrush tool and a dark brown hue.

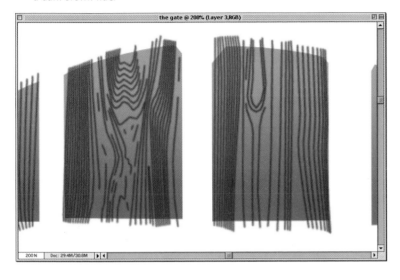

All the veins of the grain were exactly the same thickness because they were stroked in unison with the same airbrush. Real wood grain, however, is not as symmetrical. In some cases, the wood grain thickened its shape. Using the Smudge tool, I pulled out the edges of the grain to simulate the thickened grain (Figure 31).

There was a roughness to the wood of the boards that, when lit by the lantern above, seemed to take on the appearance of grooves streaming horizontally across the boards. Using the Eraser tool, with its opacity lowered just enough to give me the effect I wanted, I rendered stripes from one side of the boards to the other (Figure 32).

When I'm deciding how much to lower a tool's opacity, I try different levels. The beauty of the computer is the capability to undo what I have done. This makes experimentation a breeze.

When the grain layer was finished, I turned it into a clipping group with the boards layer and then merged them into a single layer.

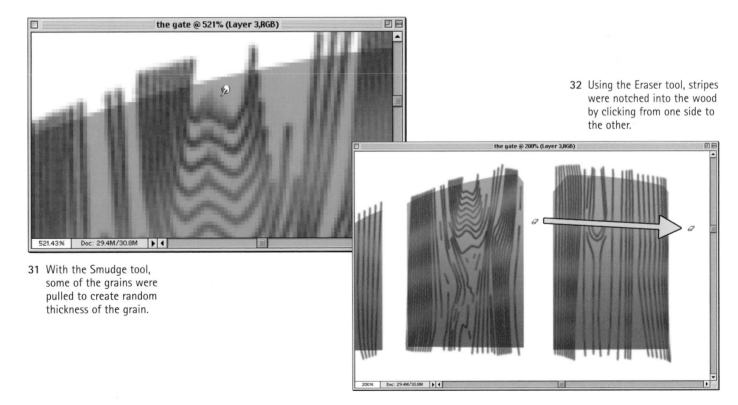

31 With the Smudge tool, some of the grains were pulled to create random thickness of the grain.

32 Using the Eraser tool, stripes were notched into the wood by clicking from one side to the other.

Playing in Some Bean Bins

Yet another type of grain can be seen in certain woods. The direction and thickness of the veins in this particular grain might be quite random. The *bean bins* image shows a variety of wood grains (Figure 33). Each of these particular wood grains was created individually.

Each area of the wooden structures was created with the Path tool. Each shape was assigned to its own layer. Then, the paths were turned into selections and filled with a basic color to represent the wood tone I needed (Figure 34).

33 The *bean bins* image shows a variety of wood textures that were created individually.

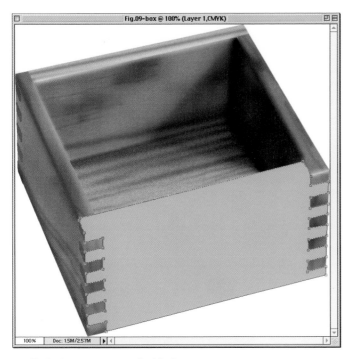

34 Each shape was created with the Path tool and filled with color in its own layer.

36 In some cases, two lines of varying size and color were created; they were then softened to appear as one stroke.

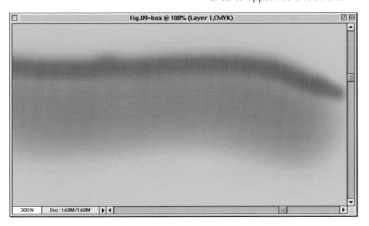

With the Airbrush tool, I added the details of the grain and nicks (Figure 35). I chose a dark color and drew thin lines for each grain, varying the size of the brush to get random grain effects.

In some cases, two adjoining lines were used: a thin dark line with a softer, lighter line added to serve as the sweep that appears in wood grains (Figure 36). Where the two lines met, I used the Smudge and Water Drop tools to soften the edge. The overall shape of the two lines was then blurred, using the Gaussian Blur filter with a setting high enough to achieve the result I was looking for. Fortunately, the filter has a preview mode, so I can experiment without wasting a great deal of time.

Some areas appear discolored by wear and age (Figure 37). To get this result, I used the Desaturate tool. This tool enables you to bring down the saturation of a color. The more you desaturate, the closer to grayscale the image becomes. Worn wood has this same desaturated look.

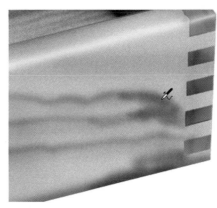

35 Strokes of the Airbrush tool simulate the wood grain.

37 Using the Desaturate tool, areas were given the appearance of the wear and tear that happens to wood that is constantly handled.

38 *handles.*

Getting into Metal

Metal is another material we see all around us. Like wood, different types of metals look different. Gold, for example, might be shiny and yellow, whereas iron could be dull and dark gray. Look at the different types of metals in the image *handles* (Figure 38).

Basic metals are fairly easy to create. First, you must create the shape or object that is made of metal. I usually do this with the Path tool. Then, you decide which metal you are going to create.

This determines the color, although that is not crucial. Because most metals look the same, you can quickly change the color of the metal by using the Hue/Saturation command. You can play alchemist and amaze your friends by turning tin into gold right before their eyes.

Let's create metal.

Exercise 7.2 Stepping through Metal

To create some metal, follow these steps:

1 In a new Illustrator file, use the Path tool to create the shape or object you want to be made of metal (Figure 39).

2 After you complete the shape, turn the path into a selection.

3 Open a new layer to house the shape and then fill the selection, using a basic color for the metal you want to illustrate (Figure 40).

- You can use a warm, golden yellow for gold, or perhaps a mid-toned gray for silver. Use the Hue/Saturation command if you want to quickly change the color of the metal.

- If your shape has roundness to it, apply a gradient rather than a flat color to start to develop the effect of the shape (Figure 41).

4 Create a new layer to contain highlights and reflections, and use the Airbrush tool to add stripes of varying sizes and color to simulate reflections and highlights caused by light sources (Figure 42).

Using an additional layer makes it easy to reposition or eliminate the reflections, as necessary.

n o t e | If the metal is polished, reflections must be sharp and almost distinguishable in nature. For additional information, see Chapter 9, "Looking at Reflections."

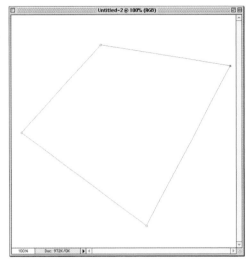

39 Using the Path tool, create the shape for the object made of metal.

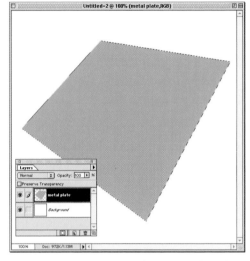

40 In a layer for the shape, fill the selection with a basic color for the metal.

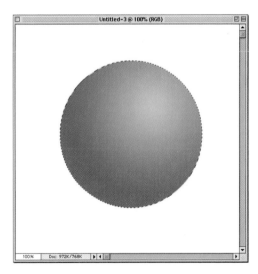

41 If the shape is round, apply a gradient to establish the roundness.

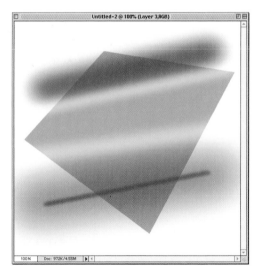

42 With the Airbrush tool, add lines of varying sizes and colors to simulate reflections on the metal.

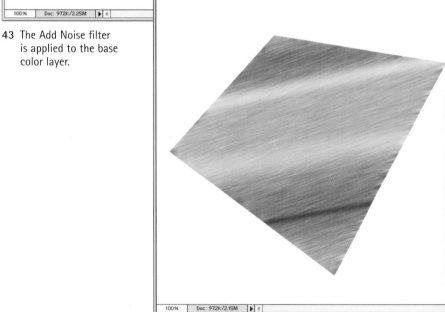

Brushed Aluminum

If you were illustrating a brushed aluminum, you would complete nearly the same process as the one in Exercise 7.2. However, you would apply a large amount of the Add Noise filter to the base color layer (Figure 43).

The Motion Blur filter is then applied to streak the noise, thus giving the appearance of brushed metal (Figure 44).

The layer containing the highlights and reflections is made visible again and then turned into a clipping group with the layer of the brushed metal texture. Finally, to have the texture show properly through highlights and reflections, the layer with highlights and reflections was put in Hardlight mode (Figure 45).

43 The Add Noise filter is applied to the base color layer.

44 The Motion Blur filter is applied to simulate the effect of brushed metal.

45 I used the Hardlight mode to make the texture show through the highlights and reflections.

158

chapter 8

Creating Textures from Patterns

In the last chapter, you saw enough wooden textures to last you for awhile. If you look around the area where you are as you read this book, you will notice other materials.

Making Metal

Metal is probably as widely used as wood. Plastic is also in there big time. The rendering, or the creation, of metal and plastic can be very similar. In many cases, they will react to light in a similar fashion. These two materials also offer the ease of introducing a patterned texture to the mix.

1 The *subway seat* image came to me one after-noon while sitting on a New York subway.

2 Upon closer inspection of the metallic area below the seat, you can see two different patterns.

Inspiration can come at any time, from anywhere. The *subway seat* image came to me one afternoon while I sat in a New York sub-way (Figure 1). What caught my eye was the intricate play between multiple textures made up of patterns.

Upon closer inspection of the metallic area below the seat, you can see two different patterns at work (Figure 2). The first is the flat, diamond-shaped texture of the metal itself. Second, you can see another pattern made by the holes cut into the metal that make up a vent system.

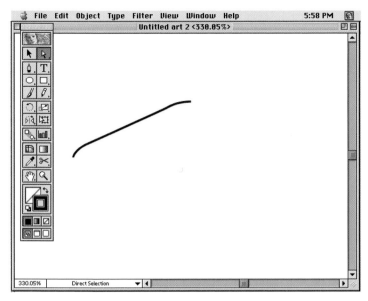

3 I used the line with curves at either end to serve as the basis for the shape of the pattern.

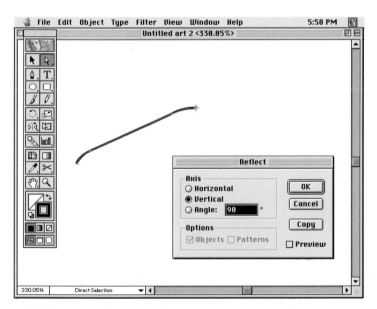

4 The line was selected and, using the Reflect tool, I copied the line on a vertical axis. Note the position of the cursor.

Creating the Metallic Texture

Creating patterns, such as the metallic texture, requires a precise positioning of elements in order to achieve a consistent look.

In Illustrator, I created a simple line with curves at either end to serve as the basis for the shape of the pattern (Figure 3). I selected the line and then, using the Reflect tool, I copied the line on a vertical axis to complete the top portion of the shape (Figure 4).

> **n o t e** | The position of the cursor is crucial when you call up the Reflect tool. When you place the cursor on the axis you want to reflect on and press the Option key on a Mac (Alt on the PC), you bring up the options dialog box for the tool. Selecting Copy in the dialog box creates a copy of the line segment, reflected on the axis chosen from the point at which the cursor rested.

The two points where the original and new lines met joined to form a single segment.

The line segment was then reflected on a horizontal axis to complete the shape. The points at which the two segments met were joined to form a single shape (Figure 5).

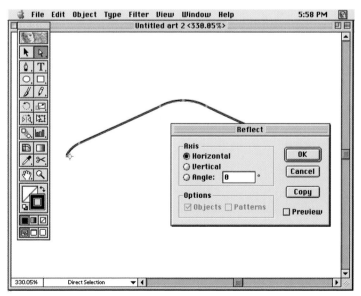

5 Notice the position of the cursor in this figure.

161

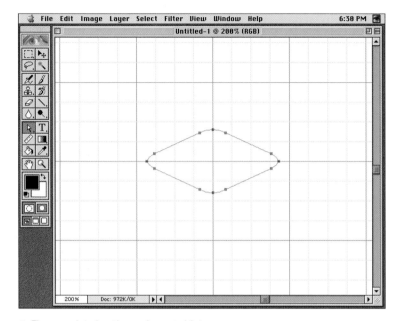

Switching to Photoshop, I opened a new blank file in which I would generate the pattern and turned on the Show Grid feature.

The completed path was imported into Photoshop as a path and saved (Figure 6). I centered it over the grid.

In a new layer, I made the path a selection and filled it with a gray tone (Figure 7). Additional shadows and highlights were added with the Airbrush tool.

6 The completed path was imported into the Photoshop file with the grid visible.

With the shape still selected, I created a series of clones and arranged them symmetrically around the original shape (Figure 8). This became the basis for the diamond-shaped pattern.

With the Rectangle selection tool and following the grid, I made a selection to encompass a section of the pattern so that the parts that were cut into were continued on the opposite side. If you look closely at Figure 9, you will notice that the shape at the top center has its top cut off. The shape at the bottom center has its top selected while its bottom is cut off. In other words, one starts where the other leaves off.

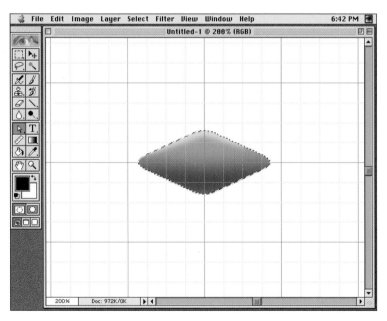

8 The shape was cloned many times to form the basis for the pattern.

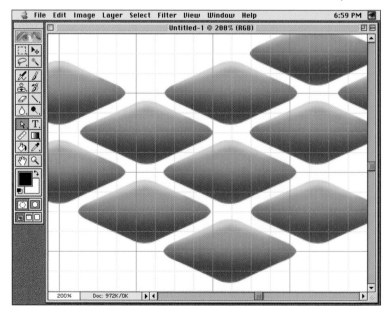

7 The path was made into a selection, and color was added.

I made sure that the eye icon for the Background layer was turned off. When the Background layer is on, white (or whatever color the layer contains) becomes part of the pattern. When the Background layer is off, the space between the shapes of the pattern is transparent.

With this area of the shapes selected, as shown in Figure 9, I defined it as a pattern (Edit>Define Pattern).

In the file that contained the art, I created a layer that contained the basic shape of the metal under the seat (Figure 10). Above it, I created a new layer that was filled with the pattern (Figure 11).

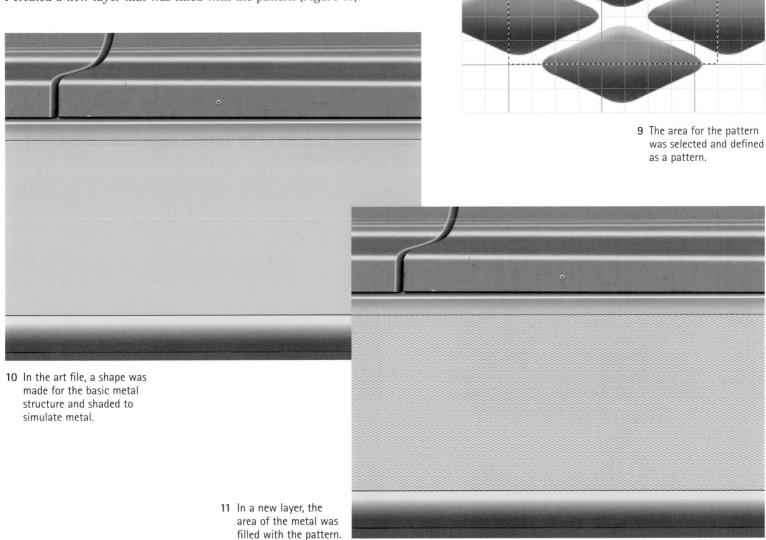

9 The area for the pattern was selected and defined as a pattern.

10 In the art file, a shape was made for the basic metal structure and shaded to simulate metal.

11 In a new layer, the area of the metal was filled with the pattern.

Cutting Holes in the Metal

The metal under the seat houses some electrical devices that require ventilation. The vent system is made of many small round holes that let the air in. To re-create this pattern, I followed the same procedure in the preceding section, but I used perfect circles as the basic shape.

Some additional details had to be added to the pattern of the holes. First, something is visible through the holes. Second, the holes were cut into the metal, and, because you are viewing them from an angle, you should see an edge that indicates the thickness of the metal (Figure 12).

In a new layer, I filled a selected area with the pattern of the holes and duplicated the layer. This additional layer was used later to add thickness to the metal (Figure 13).

In a new layer above the two layers that contained the holes, I created some shapes. Then I colored them with various hues and noise filter settings to represent the items visible through the holes (Figure 14).

I filled one of the layers that contained the holes with black, using Preserve Transparency to allow only the holes to be filled with black. This would serve as the darkness visible under the seat. The layer with the shapes was turned into a clipping group with the black-colored layer of holes (Figure 15), and then these two layers were merged into a single layer.

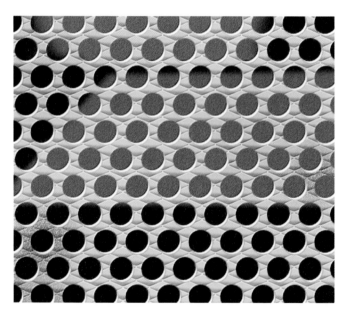

12 The holes show an edge and what is visible through them.

13 The holes copy layer shown in the Layers palette will be used later to add thickness to the metal.

14 In a new layer, some shapes were created to simulate the contents of the machinery visible through the holes.

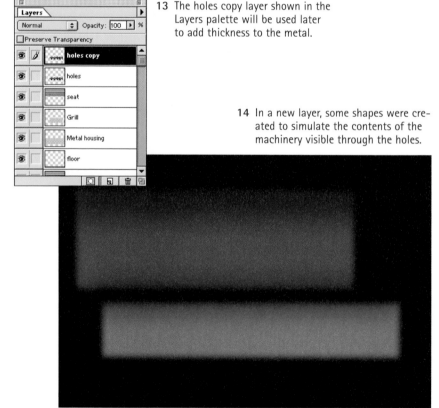

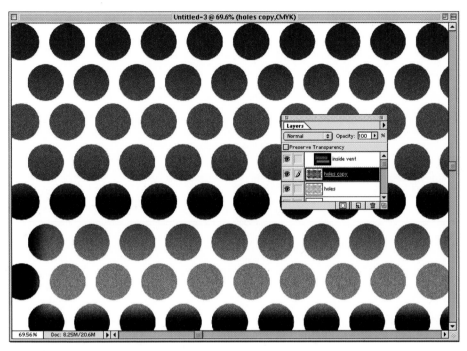

15 The layer with the machinery was clipped with the duplicate layer of holes.

The layer that contained the black holes with the machinery visible through them was then turned into a clipping group with the original layer of holes. Next, using the Move tool, I off-set slightly the layer with the black holes and shapes to show an edge made by the original holes. The layer of the original holes was filled with a gray tone to simulate a metallic materi-al. This fill was done with Preserve Trans-parency on for the layer so that only the holes would be gray. This gave the metal the appear-ance of thickness or depth when seen through the holes (Figure 16).

So there you have it—a New York subway seat re-created by using a few carefully assembled patterns.

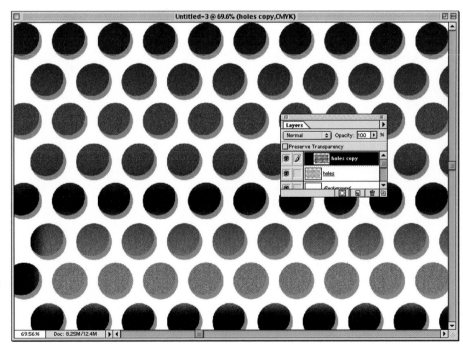

16 The merged layers of the machinery and holes were clipped with the original layer of holes and offset slightly to simulate the thickness of the metal.

Building a Brick Wall

A brick wall like the one in *Peter's Ice Cream* (Figure 17) is usually fairly symmetrical. The brick wall itself is nothing more than a shape filled with a pattern. Different bricks give a sense of randomness. The basic pattern is created using the same procedure for creating the metal texture. In fact, because the basic shapes of bricks are rectangles, this is simpler.

Let's create a brick wall together.

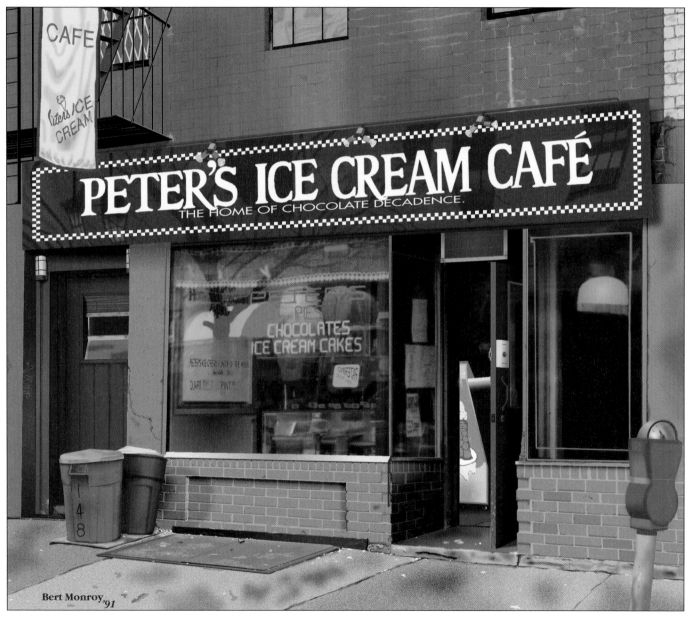

17 *Peter's Ice Cream* shows a simple red brick wall and a gray wall below the display window.

Exercise 8.1   Stepping through a Brick Wall

To create brick for your wall, follow these steps:

1 In Photoshop, create a new document that measures about 10 by 10 inches. Set the resolution to 72 dpi.

2 To make the grid visible, choose View>Show Grid and, in the Guides & Grid dialog box, set the grid subdivisions to 11 (Figure 18).

> **n o t e** | To make the creation and selection processes easy, change the grid subdivisions in the Preferences dialog box to an uneven number. The odd-numbered square in the grid reserves the space necessary for the grout between the bricks.

3 Create a new layer and zoom in so that one grid section takes up the entire screen. This will make it easier to see what you are doing.

4 With the Rectangle selection tool, select a rectangular shape that takes up 4 subdivisions down and 11 across.

5 Fill the selection with a color similar to that of a brick (Figure 19).

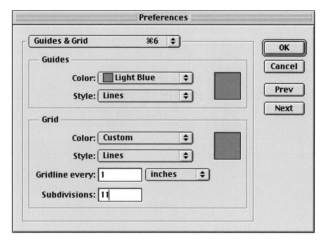

18 In the Preferences dialog box for Guides & Grid, set the subdivisions for the grid to 11.

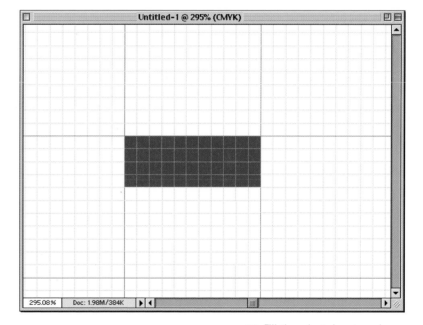

19 Fill the selected rectangular shape with a brick color.

Exercise 8.1   Stepping through a Brick Wall *(continued)*

6 Create the symmetrical pattern for the bricks by cloning the brick once to the right, leaving a single subdivision between the two bricks and then cloning the two bricks down to form the pattern (Figure 20).

n o t e | Make sure that the spacing between each brick is one subdivision. Stagger the bricks on the second row under those in the first row so that the odd subdivision of the brick is centered below the space between the bricks above, giving you a symmetrical pattern.

7 With the Rectangle selection tool, select the bricks and choose Edit>Define Pattern to turn them into a pattern. Make sure that the background is transparent. Take note of the specific area being selected in Figure 21. This selection will ensure that the pattern will be accurate. Note that where one brick leaves off, the one on the other side of the pattern picks up.

8 Once the pattern is created, deselect (Command+D on a Mac, Ctrl+D on a PC).

9 Zoom back out to 100% view and turn off the layer in which you created the pattern.

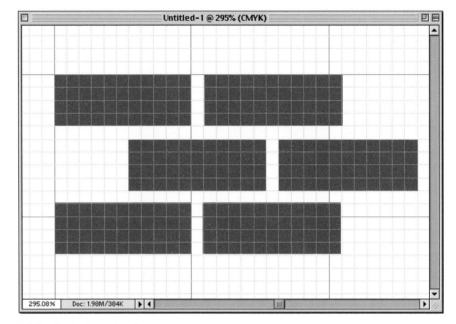

20 Duplicate the rectangle several times to form the basis of the pattern.

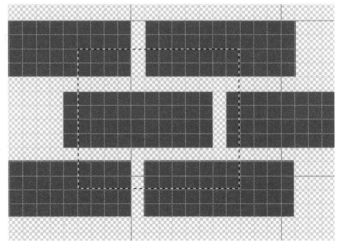

21 Select an area to encompass the entire pattern.

10 Create a new layer and fill it with the pattern of bricks. You can do this by pressing Shift+Delete or by choosing Edit>Fill> Pattern for Use.

11 Create a layer for the wall itself behind the area with the bricks and then fill the layer with the color you want the grout to be. Use the Add Noise filter in Monochromatic mode to simulate the rough quality of grout (Figure 22).

12 Select the layer with the brick pattern and choose Layers>Effects>Bevel and Emboss to add dimension to the bricks and make them look as though they are protruding from the wall (Figure 23).

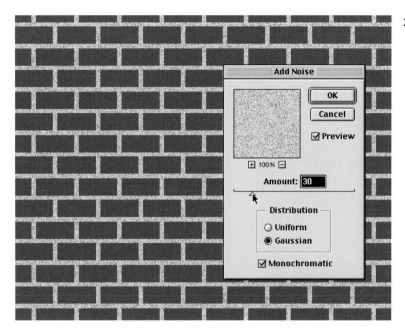

22 Fill the layer for the grout with the color you want and apply the Add Noise filter.

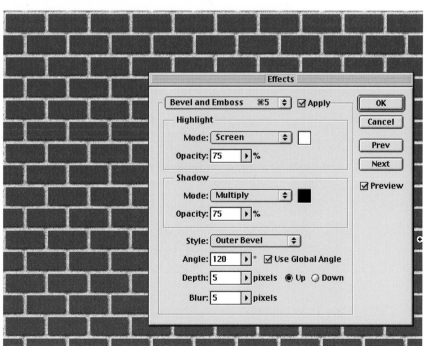

23 Apply the Bevel and Emboss to the layer of the brick pattern.

Exercise 8.1 Stepping through a Brick Wall *(continued)*

13 Use the Add Noise filter to add texture to the bricks (Figure 24).

14 Set the size of Dodge and Burn tools to the height of a brick, and dab random bricks (Figure 25).

Randomly darkening and lightening individual bricks gives the wall a more realistic look. For that extra touch, use a small airbrush with black and add a few cracks here and there.

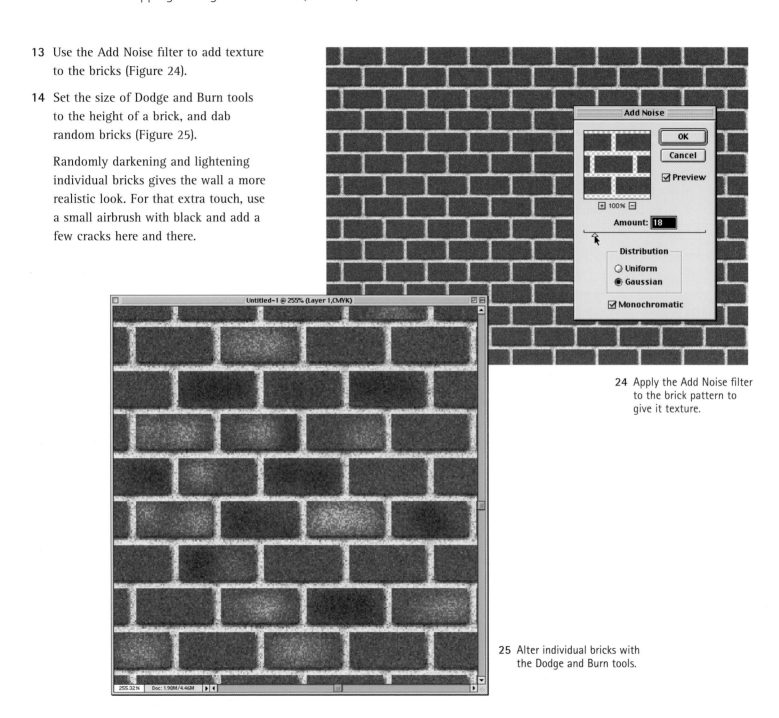

24 Apply the Add Noise filter to the brick pattern to give it texture.

25 Alter individual bricks with the Dodge and Burn tools.

Growing Some Beans

There are times when patterns can be used to fill an area, simply to save time. The *bean bins* image shows bins full of beans (Figure 26). Those beans were created as a series of patterns.

26 *bean bins.*

The beans started out as a circular selection (Figure 27).

The selection was filled with a color (Figure 28) chosen to approximate the particular type of bean.

Using the Airbrush tool, a shadow was added to give the bean a rounded look (Figure 29).

With a lighter shade of the bean color, a highlight was added (Figure 30).

27 I used a circular selection to start creating the bean.

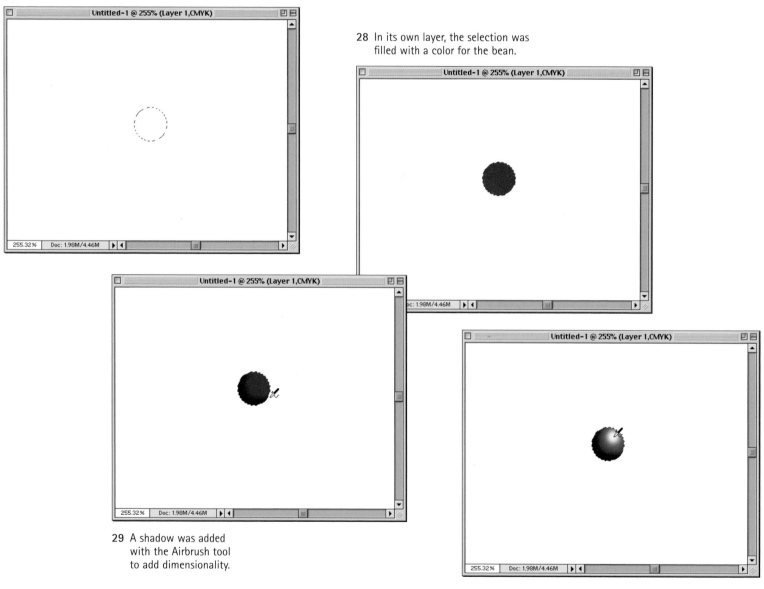

28 In its own layer, the selection was filled with a color for the bean.

29 A shadow was added with the Airbrush tool to add dimensionality.

30 A highlight was added for further dimensionality.

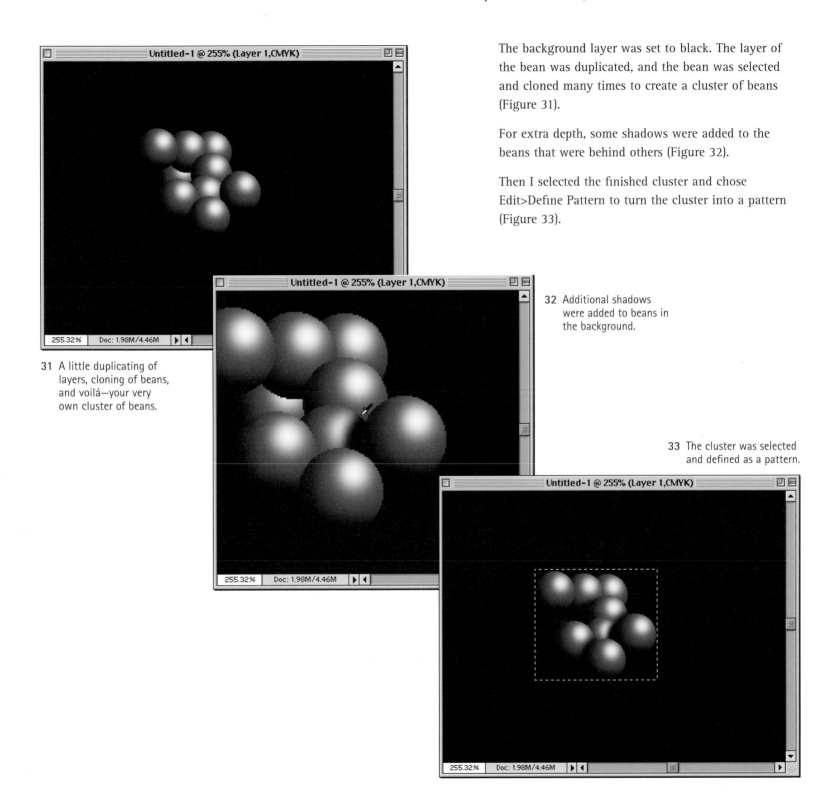

The background layer was set to black. The layer of the bean was duplicated, and the bean was selected and cloned many times to create a cluster of beans (Figure 31).

For extra depth, some shadows were added to the beans that were behind others (Figure 32).

Then I selected the finished cluster and chose Edit>Define Pattern to turn the cluster into a pattern (Figure 33).

31 A little duplicating of layers, cloning of beans, and voilá—your very own cluster of beans.

32 Additional shadows were added to beans in the background.

33 The cluster was selected and defined as a pattern.

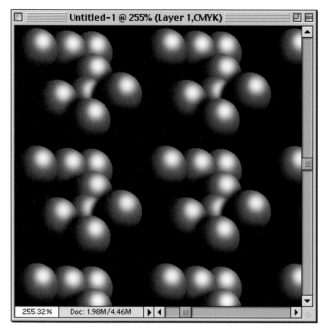

34 The new layer was filled with the pattern.

After creating a new layer to contain the pattern, I chose Fill from the Edit menu and selected Pattern for Use. The pattern of the bean clusters filled the canvas (Figure 34).

Then I brought the layer with the original bean to the foreground, over the layer with the bean pattern (Figure 35).

Additional beans were copied over areas of the pattern to break up the pattern, making it look as if all the beans were randomly placed (Figure 36). Additional shadows were painted over the pattern to accommodate the new beans.

The same technique was used for the each type of bean. The result is a realistic image of a bean stall at a market.

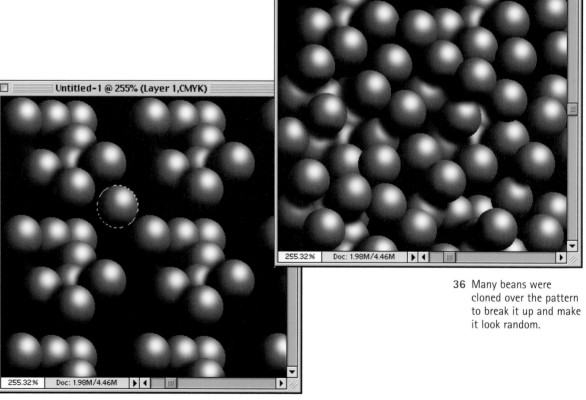

35 The original layer of the single bean was brought to the foreground, and the bean was selected.

36 Many beans were cloned over the pattern to break it up and make it look random.

Making Rain

Rain can be re-created by using patterns. That's right! I said *rain*.
In *The construction site*, for example, it's raining (Figure 37).

37 *The construction site.*

Let me take you back a few steps before
the rain. I used a filter to create the cloudy
sky, chose a black and a deep reddish-blue
for my foreground and background colors,
and then simply applied the Clouds filter
(Filter>Render>Clouds) to the Background
layer (Figure 38).

Using the Airbrush tool, I added a little
more black tone along the top and a little
more blue along the bottom (Figure 39).
Just a small adjustment to make it look
more like a real sky.

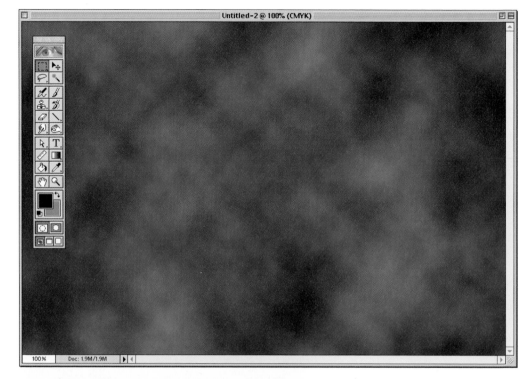

38 With black as the foreground color and a dark
blue as the background
color, the Clouds filter
was applied.

39 To add realism, a little
adjustment to the sky
was done with the
Airbrush tool.

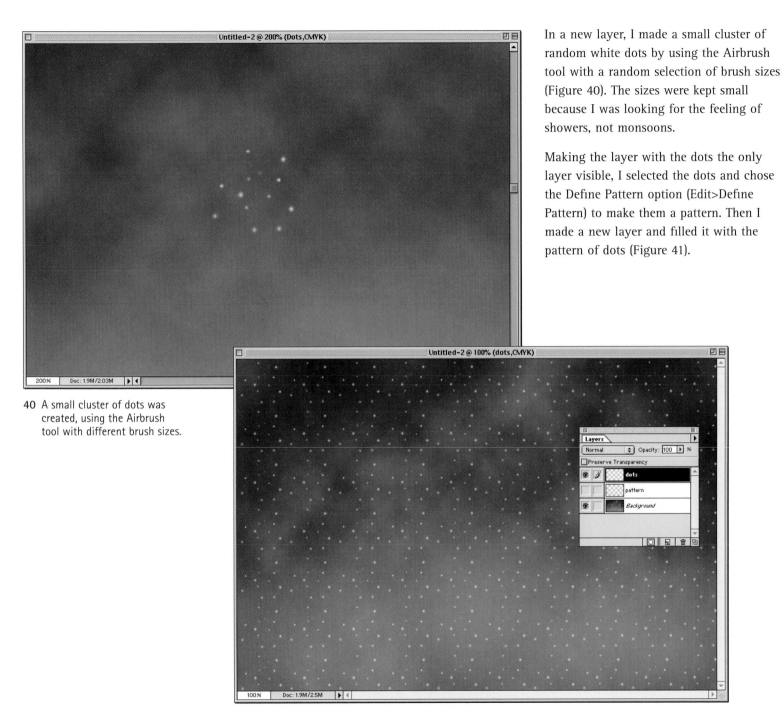

In a new layer, I made a small cluster of random white dots by using the Airbrush tool with a random selection of brush sizes (Figure 40). The sizes were kept small because I was looking for the feeling of showers, not monsoons.

Making the layer with the dots the only layer visible, I selected the dots and chose the Define Pattern option (Edit>Define Pattern) to make them a pattern. Then I made a new layer and filled it with the pattern of dots (Figure 41).

40 A small cluster of dots was created, using the Airbrush tool with different brush sizes.

41 The dot pattern was used to fill a new layer.

177

In the layer with the original dots, I made another cluster (Figure 42) and then followed the same steps and made it a pattern.

I made another layer and filled it with the second dot pattern (Figure 43).

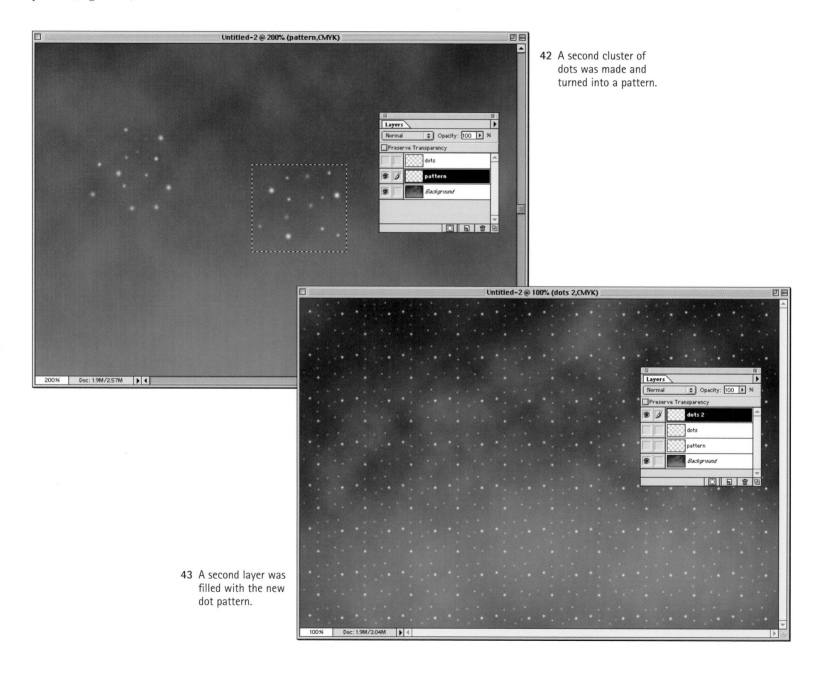

42 A second cluster of dots was made and turned into a pattern.

43 A second layer was filled with the new dot pattern.

Next, after making all layers visible, I applied the Motion Blur filter to one of the dot layers at an angle to suggest wind (Figure 44). The distance was set to a number that would simulate the rainfall.

Then Motion Blur filter was applied to the other dot layer, but with a different distance (Figure 45). Look out! Get your umbrellas!

44 The Motion Blur filter was applied to one of the dot layers.

45 The Motion Blur filter was applied to the other dot layer.

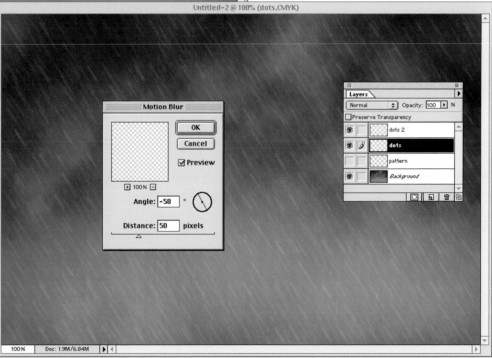

46 *Cedar*.

Pouring a Sidewalk

Now that we have rain pouring down, wouldn't it be nice to have some ground for it to fall on?

You might remember an image, called *Cedar*, from an earlier chapter. Take a second and look at it again. In the foreground is a narrow concrete sidewalk, flanked by trenches filled with dirt and weeds (Figures 46 and 47).

Sidewalks are easy to create! Of course, if you think about it, the material can be used for stone walls or any surface made of stone.

Let's try our hand at digitally pouring a sidewalk.

47 This is a close-up view of the ground area of the image

Exercise 8.2 Stepping on a Sidewalk

To create a sidewalk, follow these steps:

1 Select the area for the sidewalk (or block, or other stone surface), as shown in Figure 48.

2 Fill the area with a gray tone (Figure 49).

3 Apply the Add Noise filter in Monochrome mode. Note that the value in Figure 50 is just enough to add some roughness to the texture.

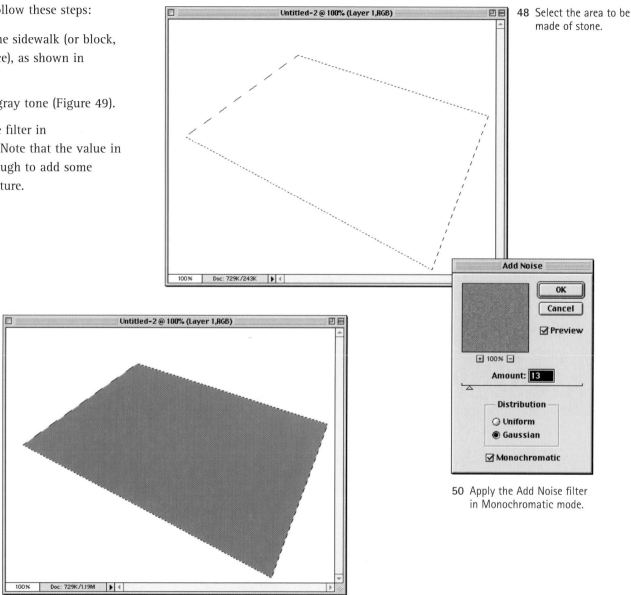

48 Select the area to be made of stone.

50 Apply the Add Noise filter in Monochromatic mode.

49 Fill the area with a gray tone.

Exercise 8.2 Stepping on a Sidewalk *(continued)*

4 With a tiny Airbrush tool, add a few cracks here and there (Figure 51). With the Dodge and Burn tools, give the area a dab in a few places to lighten and darken the stone for a more random effect.

5 Select the area and fill it with brown. Give the old Add Noise filter a value low enough to add just a touch of graininess, as you did in the stone of the previous exercise. So far, this is just like the stone texture, except for the color.

6 Apply the Craquelure filter (Filter>Texture>Craquelure), as shown in Figure 52.

Your groundwork, so to speak, is done. A few details will enhance the overall look of the ground—a few rocks here and there for soil areas, and an occasional ground-in wad of chewing gum or a cigarette butt will add realism to the sidewalk.

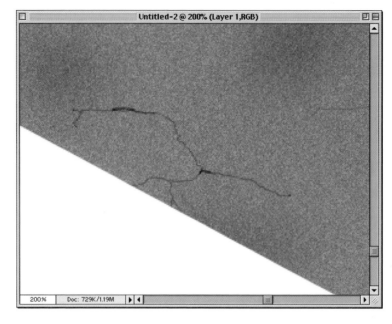

51 Add a few cracks and dark tones here and there for realism.

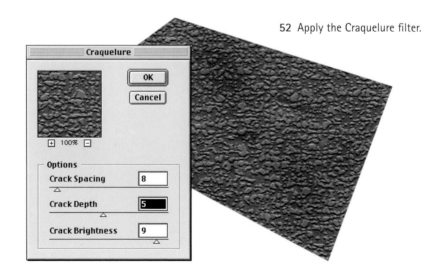

52 Apply the Craquelure filter.

chapter 9

Looking at Reflections

Up to now, we have created all types of objects and the materials those objects are made of. In Chapter 4, "Shading," you saw how objects cast shadows or have shadows cast onto them. There is another aspect to a materials surface that needs to be addressed. The grand finale for portraying these objects and their materials is to interpret how they react to the world around them.

For example, take a wooden table from one of those raw wood furniture places—easy to reproduce with the techniques of the "Working with Wood and Metal" chapter. Apply a little polish to that table and what happens? Suddenly, you can see yourself in it.

In this, the final chapter, we will explore many of the different forms that reflections can take.

Understanding Reflections

Reflections give a different dimension to an object. A diamond without reflections would not look like a diamond. It would look like a dull fake. Likewise, if a surface you are creating is polished, it has to reflect its surroundings in order to look polished.

A reflection is basically an object flipped in the opposite direction from which it is being viewed. You may be thinking, "Why not just take an image and choose Flip Horizontal from the Edit>Transform menu?" In some cases, that method is all that is necessary, but often it just doesn't give you the best results. Usually, there are other factors involved. The shape of the reflective object, for example, is a major consideration. Angles will distort the reflection. Remember the mirrors in the Fun House at the amusement park?

On a Round Surface

The marble in the painting *matches and marble* is picking up a reflection of the matchstick next to it (Figure 1). The marble is made of a smooth glass that acts as a mirror. It has a rounded surface, a shape that will distort any reflection.

The Spherize filter has been part of Photoshop's filters collection since the early versions of the program. Basically, this filter bloats the central part of an image or selected area. It creates the illusion of wrapping the image around a sphere. The appropriate distortion is applied to the edges to give the foreshortening needed to complete the roundness of the object. In Figure 2, you see a before and after example of the effect of the Spherize filter.

1 This close-up of the marble from the *marble and matches* image shows the reflection of the matchstick on the side of the marble.

2 The image on the left is the original. The one on the right has had the Spherize filter applied to it. Note the distortion of the edges. The background on the right was darkened to emphasize the effect for this example.

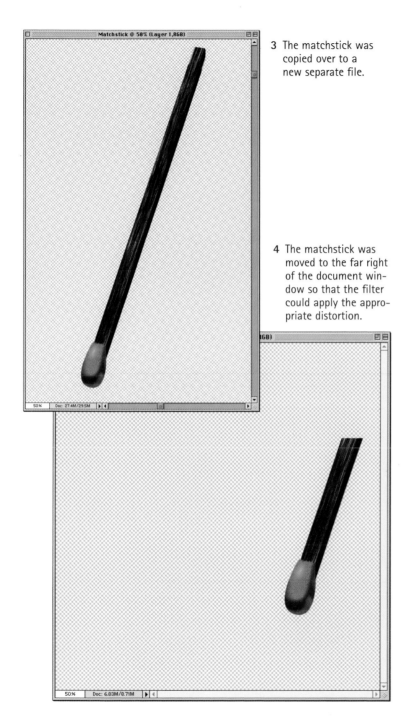

3 The matchstick was copied over to a new separate file.

4 The matchstick was moved to the far right of the document window so that the filter could apply the appropriate distortion.

This distortion of the edges is the effect I needed for the matchstick on the side of the marble.

I took the layer that contained the matchstick and duplicated it over to a new file (Figure 3). It was necessary to keep the matchstick in a layer so that the file would not be flattened.

The Spherize filter creates a sphere that is centered within the image. Knowing that the marble was a perfect sphere, I made the canvas of the file containing the matchstick a perfect square so that I could guarantee that the distortion matched the shape of the marble. Because the reflection of the matchstick would appear on the right edge of the marble, I needed the distortion to appear along the right edge. To accomplish this, I placed the layer containing the matchstick to the far right of the window (Figure 4).

The Spherize filter was called into action (Filter>Distort>Spherize). I gave it the full amount, applying it twice to maximize the effect (Figure 5).

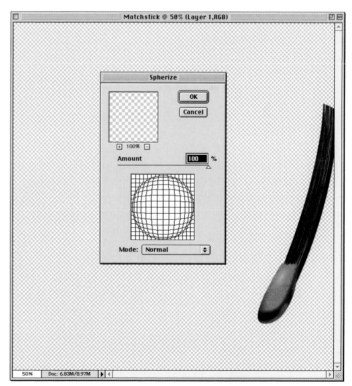

5 The Spherize filter was applied to the layer of the matchstick.

Then I scaled down the width of the distorted matchstick (Figure 6) to give it the additional distortion needed for realism.

I brought the layer with the distorted matchstick into the file with the marble (Figure 7), placing the match layer above the layer containing the marble so that the matchstick would be visible over the marble. The matchstick was rotated and scaled further to fall into the position where I wanted the reflection to appear.

The layers of the marble and matchstick were turned into a clipping group (Figure 8). Because the layer of the marble was below the layer of the match, its transparency information masked out the unwanted sections of the matchstick.

The opacity of the matchstick layer was lowered to allow the color of the marble to show through (Figure 9).

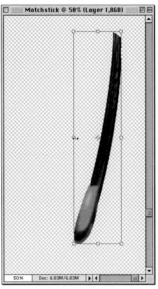

6 The matchstick was scaled down to make it look thinner.

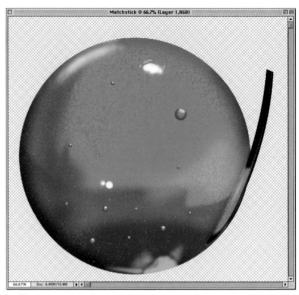

7 The layer with the matchstick was copied over to the file with the marble.

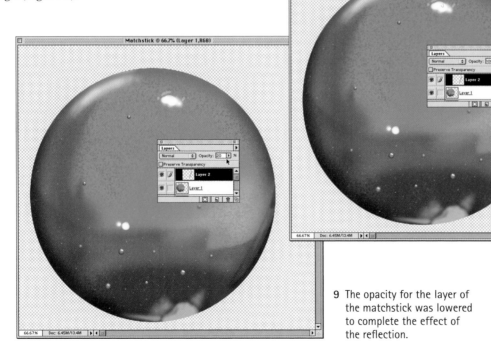

8 The layer with the matchstick and the layer of the marble were turned into a clipping group.

9 The opacity for the layer of the matchstick was lowered to complete the effect of the reflection.

Out a Window

A variety of effects can be applied to windows on buildings and storefronts to make them look real. The occasional streak of light is good, but to make them believable, reflections need to be added.

In the days before layers, reflections on storefront windows were quite difficult to do. The reflections visible in the window of

Peter's Ice Cream were created by actually painting each one in as a blend with the interior of the cafe (Figure 10). I actually mixed colors as I went along to create the effect. Layers changed all that.

Today, reflections can be a very easy task—no fancy distortion tricks like the ones I used for the marble. Easy, if the scene being reflected is not visible within the area of the image.

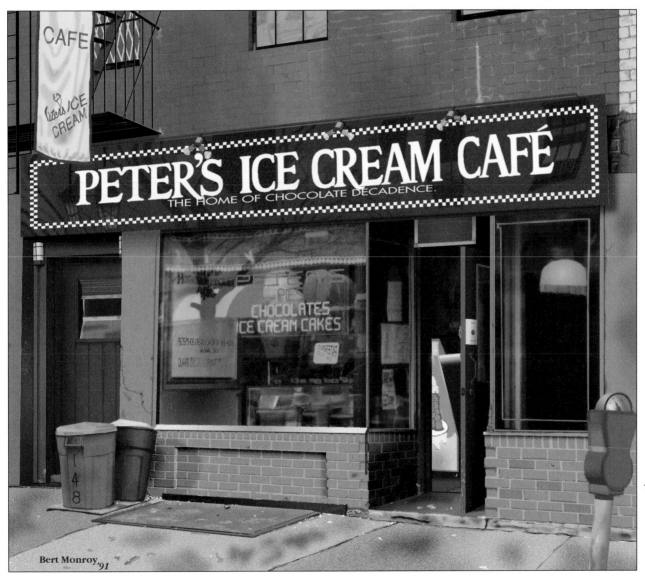

10 The reflections in the window of *Peter's Ice Cream* were painted right on the background. This image was painted before the introduction of layers.

187

Figure 11 shows another of my paintings, *The Raven*, with a close-up of the theater window. The area of the window was in its own layer. A scaled-down version of *Pic-n-Pac* was imported into the image of the theater and put into a clipping group with the layer of the window. The opacity for the layer of the reflection (*Pic-n-Pac*) was lowered to soften its effect.

The painting *Pic-n-Pac* has a multitude of reflections visible within its windows (Figure 12). These reflections were created individually.

Each reflection was created in a separate layer. Figure 13 shows the detail of the reflection visible in the first window on the left.

The image of the reflection is a rough drawing created with the Paintbrush tool and a variety of brush sizes and colors. The subject of that reflection is none other than yours truly, standing in the middle of the street, taking the picture (Figure 14). I did not need any details because the final effect would be almost invisible.

The process of creating a reflection is simple. Let's create one together.

11 The close-up, showing the detail of the reflection in the window, shows the use of the painting *Pic-n-Pac* as the reflection.

.

.

.

13 The close-up, showing the detail of the reflection in the window, demonstrates the use of another painting as the reflection.

12 *Pic-n-Pac.*

14 The close-up of the reflection in the windows is actually a rough drawing of me holding my camera.

Exercise 9.1   Stepping through a Reflection

To create a reflection, follow these steps:

1 Open an image with a window in which you want to show a reflection (Figure 15).

2 Select the area of the window and copy it to a separate layer (Layer>New>Layer via copy) (Figure 16).

15 Open an image in which a window is clearly visible.

16 Select the area of the window and copy it to a separate layer.

3 Open a second image that contains what you want the reflection to be (Figure 17).

4 Using the Move tool, drag the reflection image over to the image with the window and then create a clipping group with the layer of the window (Figure 18).

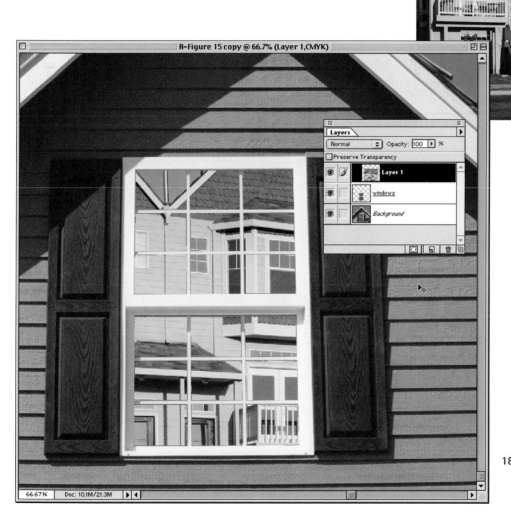

17 Open a second image that will serve as the reflection.

18 Create a clipping group with the layer of the window and the layer of the reflection.

Exercise 9.1 Stepping through a Reflection *(continued)*

5 Using the Move tool, position the reflection exactly where you want it (Figure 19).

6 Lower the opacity of the layer with the reflection to a percentage you like (Figure 20). That's all there is to it!

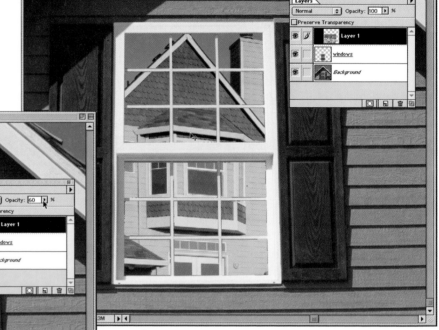

19 Position the reflection where you want it within the area of the window.

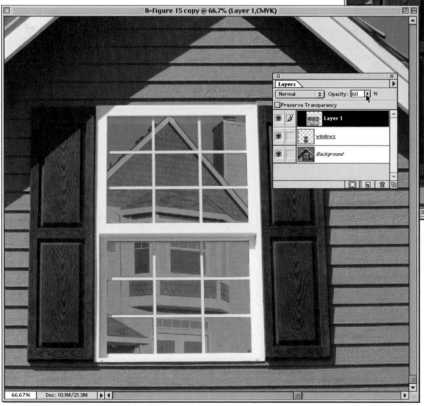

20 Lower the opacity of the layer with the reflection.

21 *Akihabara.*

On Plastic

The painting *Akihabara* concentrates on a storefront in the electronics district of Tokyo (Figure 21). The store's entire exterior was festooned with signs.

I want to draw your attention to the sign, made of big plastic letters, just below the awning (Figure 22). Without reflections, the letters would not look like plastic.

The reflections were created by painting with the Airbrush tool within a selected area. First, in a layer above the layer that contained the letters, I selected an oval with the Elliptical selection tool (Figure 23).

Then, using the Airbrush tool, I added streaks of white along the edges and down the front. These touches were the reflection of the light bouncing off the inside of the lampshade (Figure 24).

I added a single hot spot to represent the reflection of the light bulb inside the lamp (Figure 25).

When the reflection was complete, I lowered the opacity of the layer so that it would blend with the letters of the sign.

22 Reflections give the letters the look of shiny, reflective plastic.

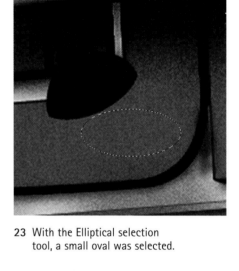

23 With the Elliptical selection tool, a small oval was selected.

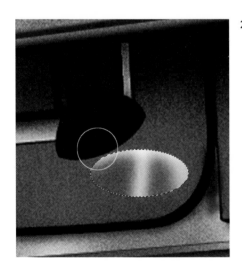

24 With the Airbrush tool, little highlights were added to represent the reflection of the light within the lampshade.

25 An additional hot spot was created with the Airbrush tool to be the reflection of the light bulb.

On Metal

If you take a close look at the spotlights visible above the awning, you can see that they are made of a very shiny metal. This shininess is made possible by adding reflections to the surface (Figure 26).

The shapes for the spots were created with the Path tool. The paths were made into selections and filled with a solid color (Figure 27).

I selected Preserve Transparency for the layer of the spots. Then, using various hues and the Airbrush and Paintbrush tools, I added shapes to represent reflections (Figure 28).

This particular procedure will be further explored in the next section.

26 The spotlights above the awning are made of a shiny metal.

27 The shapes for the spotlights were filled with a solid color.

28 Reflections were then added to the spotlights.

On Handles

The *handles* image is the filing cabinet directly below the counter that holds my computers (Figure 29). I was looking for something to paint one day during the rainy season. I laid my head down on the counter—and there I was, staring down at my next painting!

29 *handles.*

Looking at close-ups of the handle areas for the top (Figure 30) and bottom (figure 31), you can see that a configuration of strange shapes makes up the reflections.

The odd angle of the handles and their slim curved surfaces made for an interesting study of reflections.

30 This is a close-up of the top handle of the filing cabinet under my desk.

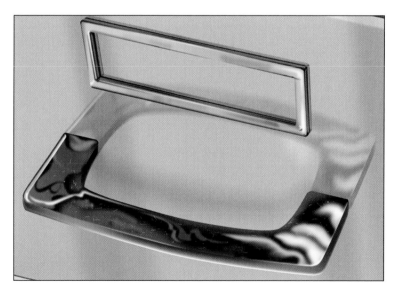

31 This is a close-up of the bottom handle of the filing cabinet.

The shapes of the handles were created in Photoshop, using the Path tool (Figure 32).

In a separate layer for each handle, the paths were made into selections and filled with a solid gray color (Figure 33). I used a gray that was predominant in the overall color of the handle.

Preserve Transparency was selected for the layers of the handles. Using the Airbrush tool, I sprayed soft highlights along the edges with various shades of light gray (Figure 34).

With the Path tool, wavy shapes were created to simulate the distorted patterns I saw in the actual handles (Figure 35). These paths were made into selections with varying feather amounts to soften the edges. The selections were then filled with appropriate colors. In some cases, the selections were filled with gradients to create a sweeping highlight.

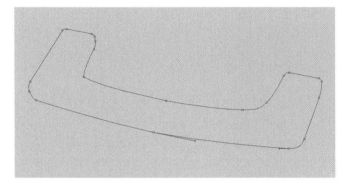

32 Shapes for the handles were created in Photoshop with the Path tool.

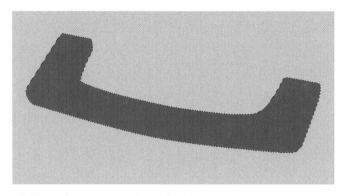

33 The paths were turned into selections and filled with a solid color.

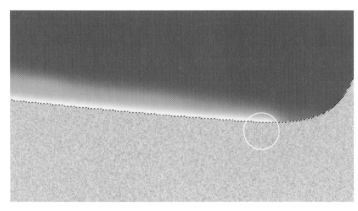

34 With the Airbrush, highlights were added to the edges of the handles.

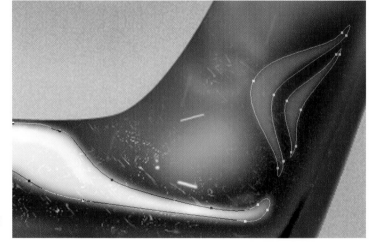

35 Shapes for the various highlights were created with the Path tool.

Some of the shapes for the highlights were further distorted with the Smudge tool (Figure 36).

Dust and scratches were added in a separate layer with the Paintbrush tool.

When each of the handles was completed, all the layers that pertained to it were merged into a single layer. This merged layer was duplicated. The duplicate was to serve as the basis for the reflection of the handle on the face of the cabinet drawer.

The reflection layer was flipped, rotated, and skewed to follow the direction of the original handle (Figure 37). This made a mirror image of the handle.

To match up the position of the reflected handle against the original handle, more distortion was necessary. I used the Distort feature (Edit>Transform>Distort) to add it (Figure 38).

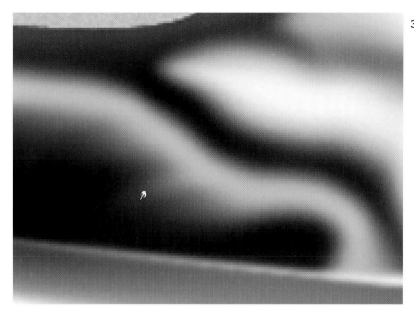

36 Some of the highlights were further distorted with the Smudge tool.

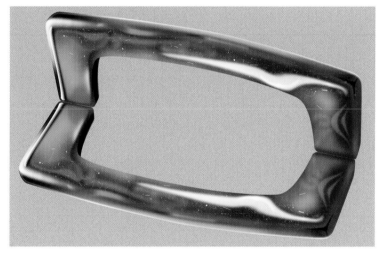

37 The duplicate handle was flipped, rotated, and skewed to match the angle of the original handle.

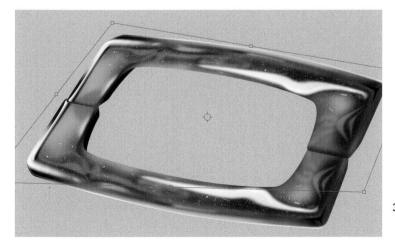

38 Some additional distortion was required to properly match the position of the reflection.

The layer with the reflection was given a slight Motion Blur filter to soften the effect with a little streaking to the edges.

The opacity was then lowered for the layer. Finally, a layer mask was applied to make the reflection fade out as it got further from the face of the drawer (Figure 39).

The creation of shapes to represent distorted reflections can also denote the actual shape of the object.

The glass applicator in the *ointment* image is a prime example of this technique (Figure 40). In this case, the reflections outline the shape. Without reflections, the applicator would appear to be a flat, solid spoon.

39 The opacity was lowered and a layer mask was applied to fade out the reflection.

On the Glory Shot

A *glory shot* is a photograph that draws attention to, or spotlights, a product. Look at any magazine ad for a product to see what I mean.

Many a time I have been commissioned to create a glory shot of a product that is still in the planning stage. Nothing can be photographed because the product doesn't exist yet. Other times, I am given a straight-on, boring shot and asked to make it dramatic. Placing that object on a reflective surface is a trick photographers use frequently.

In Figure 41, the art for a video package is flat because it is intended to be used for reproduction. Figure 42 shows how I have transformed the flat art into a three-dimensional image. The procedure I used is outlined in the chapter on perspective.

40 The glass applicator was made with many different paths that were filled with varying colors.

42 The flat art was transformed into a three-dimensional box.

We are going to do a glory shot together in the next exercise. You have two options of what to use as a product:

- You can scan a box of a product you have. Scan the front and the spine. Follow the exercise in the chapter on perspective to make it three-dimensional.

- Scan a product box from a mail-order catalog. Look through any computer products catalog—you will find hundreds of boxes available.

When you make the scan, keep the resolution low. This is just an exercise and will not be going to press. This way you will not be taxing RAM, and things will progress quickly.

Now we are going to create the glory shot for our product.

41 The art for the video package is flat art for reproduction.

Exercise 9.2   Stepping through the Glory Shot

To create a glory shot, follow these steps:

1 In the file with your product, separate the box from the back-ground, place it in its own layer, and size the file so that the height of the box is approximately six inches (Figure 43).

2 In Photoshop, create a new document that measures about 10 inches square and set the resolution at 72 ppi (Figure 44).

   This relatively small document should make your work easy.

3 Select the upper half of the window (Figure 45).

4 Fill the selection with a gradient of deep blue to light blue, as shown in Figure 46.

43 Scan a product and resize it so that it is six inches high. Separate the box from the background.

44 In Photoshop, create a new file with the settings shown here.

45 Select the upper half of the window.

46 Fill the selected area with a deep blue to light-blue gradient.

202

5 Choose Inverse (Select>Inverse) to select the lower half (Figure 47).

6 Fill the lower half with a gradient of black to deep blue, as shown in Figure 48.

7 Switch over to the file that contains the product shot. Select the layer with the product and drag it over to the file with the gradient backgrounds. The product will automatically fall into its own layer (Figure 49).

8 Position the product so that it is at the top of the window (Figure 50).

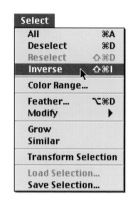

47 Choose Inverse from the Select menu.

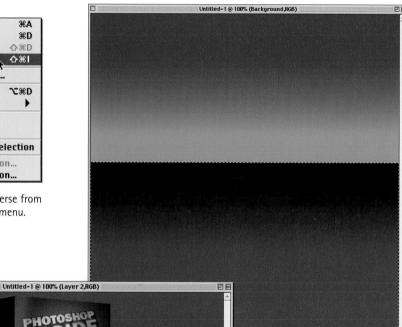

48 Fill the selected area with a black to deep-blue gradient.

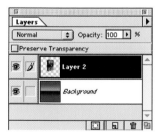

49 Import the layer of the product into the new file with the gradient fills.

50 Place the product at the top of the window.

Exercise 9.2 Stepping through the Glory Shot *(continued)*

9 Duplicate the layer of the product (Figure 51).

10 Flip the layer vertically (Edit>Transform> Flip Vertical), as shown in Figure 52.

11 Move the flipped layer so that the point of the box touches the same point on the original box (Figure 53).

12 In the layer of the flipped box, select the right side (front) of the box (Figure 54).

n o t e | If the image you scanned is facing in the opposite direction, then switch your orientation in following this exercise.

51 Duplicate the layer with the product.

52 Flip the duplicate product layer vertically.

53 Reposition the flipped copy so that the point of the edge butts up against the point of the original box.

54 Select the right side of the box.

13 Using the Skew function (Edit>Transform>Skew), skew the right edge of the selection so that the top edge of the selection matches the bottom edge of the original box (Figure 55).

14 Select the left side (spine) of the box (Figure 56).

15 As in step 13, use the Skew function (Edit>Transform>Skew) to skew the left edge of the selection so that the top edge of the selection matches the bottom edge of the original box (Figure 57).

57 Skew the left side of the selection to match the top of the selected area to the bottom of the original box.

56 Select the left side of the box.

55 Skew the right side of the selection to match the top of the selected area to the bottom of the original box.

205

Exercise 9.2 Stepping through the Glory Shot *(continued)*

16 Lower the opacity for the layer of the reflection (Figure 58).

17 Choose Layer>Add Layer Mask>Reveal All to add a layer mask to the reflection layer (Figure 59).

18 In the layer mask, create a gradient from black at the bottom of the reflection, to white, a short distance from the top edge. This will hide the lower part of the reflection (Figure 60).

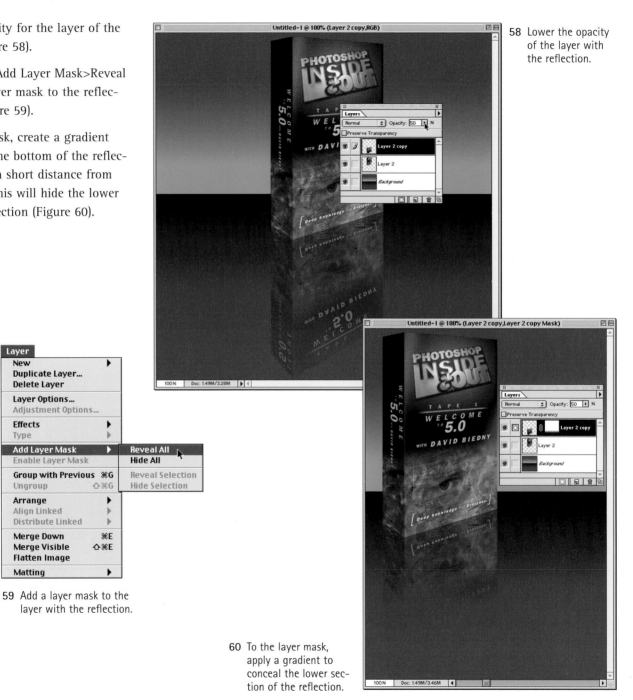

58 Lower the opacity of the layer with the reflection.

59 Add a layer mask to the layer with the reflection.

60 To the layer mask, apply a gradient to conceal the lower section of the reflection.

19 Link the layer of the reflection to the layer containing the original box so that you will be able to move them simultaneously (Figure 61).

20 With the Move tool, move the two layers so that they are centered within the document. You have now completed your "glory shot" (Figure 62).

61 Link the layer with the reflection to the layer of the original box.

62 The completed "glory shot."

Exceptions to the Rule

The procedure outlined in Exercise 9.2 can be used in many instances. At times, however, some additional steps are necessary to achieve a realistic-looking effect.

63 The reflection in this example is a copy of the ball, flipped vertically and with the opacity lowered.

The box had a flat surface that made creating a reflection fairly easy to do. Some objects are not so easy. A ball placed on a reflective surface, for example, is going to create a different reflection. The surface of the ball is rounded, so as it rests on a plane, the viewer will be able to see the underside of the ball reflected. Duplicating the layer and flipping it will not look right. Figure 63 shows what happens if flipping is all that you do.

Figure 64 shows the proper way to create the reflection. Notice that the angles of the color bands in the reflection are in the opposite direction from the ones in the ball. The opacity was lowered the same amount as in Figure 63.

In Figure 65, the reflection has a layer mask applied. A Motion Blur filter was also applied through an alpha channel that exposed the bottom half of the reflection.

64 The reflection in this example is a completely new ball that has different gradients running through it.

65 The reflection has been subjected to additional effects to add realism.

Reflections on a Commercial Project

There are other instances in which the reflection must be tweaked to get it right. The image in Figure 66 is a composite of multiple images that I was commissioned to create. The client also requested a nicer floor for the unit to stand on.

66 This image, a composite of multiple images, was commissioned for a catalog cover.

67 This is the image for the cover in its original form.

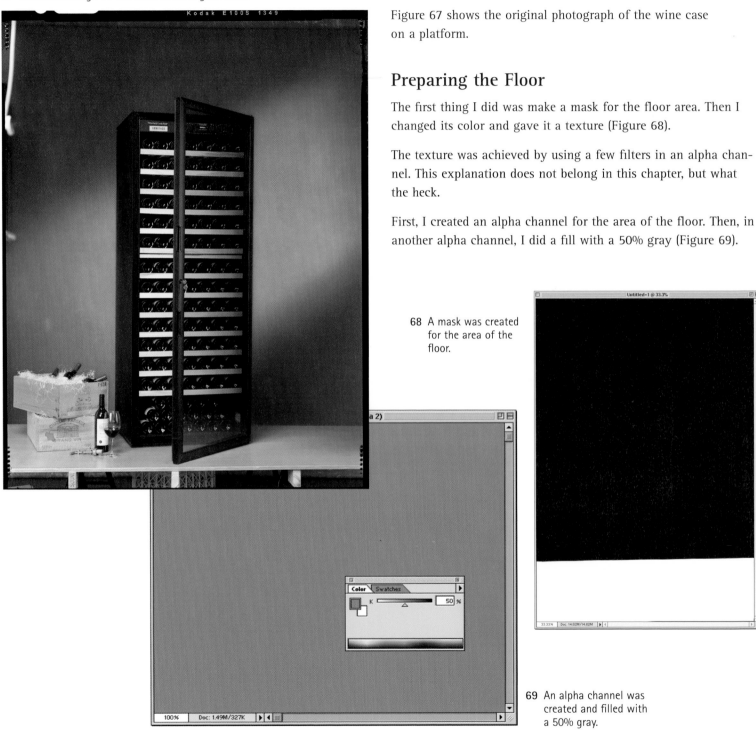

Figure 67 shows the original photograph of the wine case on a platform.

Preparing the Floor

The first thing I did was make a mask for the floor area. Then I changed its color and gave it a texture (Figure 68).

The texture was achieved by using a few filters in an alpha channel. This explanation does not belong in this chapter, but what the heck.

First, I created an alpha channel for the area of the floor. Then, in another alpha channel, I did a fill with a 50% gray (Figure 69).

68 A mask was created for the area of the floor.

69 An alpha channel was created and filled with a 50% gray.

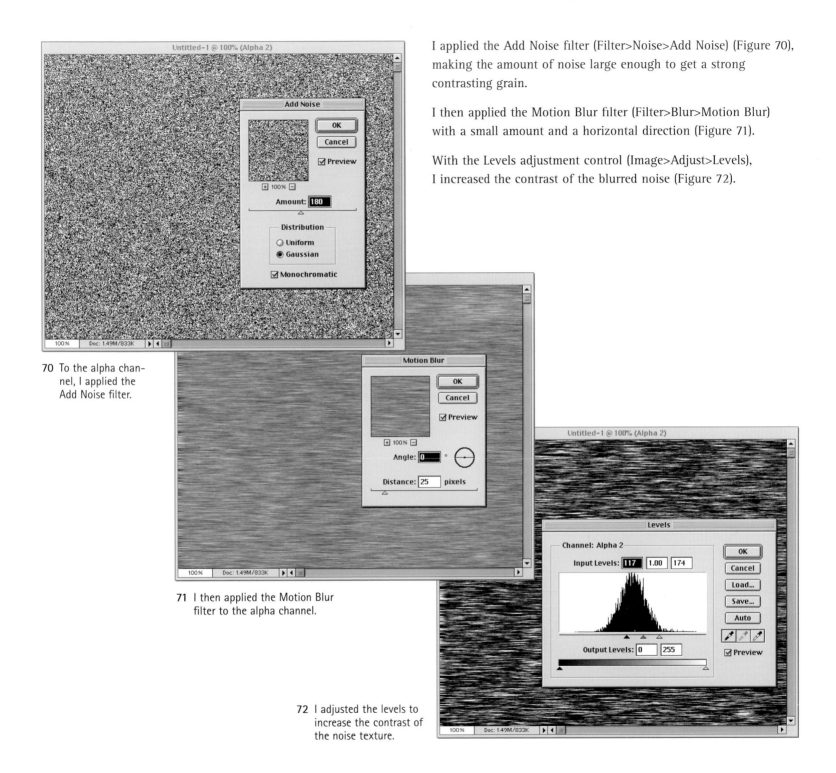

I applied the Add Noise filter (Filter>Noise>Add Noise) (Figure 70), making the amount of noise large enough to get a strong contrasting grain.

I then applied the Motion Blur filter (Filter>Blur>Motion Blur) with a small amount and a horizontal direction (Figure 71).

With the Levels adjustment control (Image>Adjust>Levels), I increased the contrast of the blurred noise (Figure 72).

70 To the alpha chan-
nel, I applied the
Add Noise filter.

71 I then applied the Motion Blur
filter to the alpha channel.

72 I adjusted the levels to
increase the contrast of
the noise texture.

With the Calculations command (Image>Calculations), I created a new alpha channel that took the channel with the texture I had created and combined it with the alpha channel for the area of the floor (Figure 73).

Returning to the Color space, I applied the alpha channel for the textured floor as a selection. In a new layer to contain the texture, I filled the selection with black. I lowered the opacity and changed the layer's mode to Multiply, and the floor was nearly done.

In Figure 74, the floor has been put in place. An additional effect was added here—a dark gradient that darkens the floor as it recedes.

Next came the reflections.

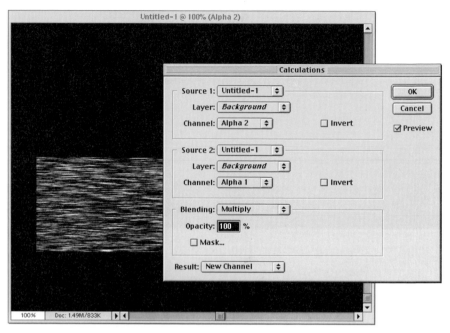

73 The Calculations command was used to create an alpha channel that combined the texture channel with the one of the area for the floor.

74 The layer of the floor was created.

Adding the Reflections

Basically, the method used to create the reflections in this image was very similar to the procedure you followed in the glory shot exercise.

The two wine crates are stacked on top of each other. They are not stacked evenly and therein lies the problem. What is happening here is similar to what happened in the image of the ball. You see an underside. The top crate has an underside that should be visible in the reflection.

I'll walk you through the procedure so you can see the methods I used to create the final image.

I created an alpha channel to separate the crates, wine cabinet, and other objects from the background. Figure 75 shows a close-up of the area in the alpha channel for the crates and the bottle opener.

75 An alpha channel was created for all the objects in the image. Here you see a close-up of the area of the wine crates and bottle opener.

I placed the layer with all the objects in front of the layer of the floor (Figure 76) to create the sensation of the objects resting on the floor.

76 The layer with the objects was placed in front of the floor layer.

213

The wine goblet and the bottle opener were placed in a layer of their own (Figure 77). This layer was duplicated and flipped vertically. The bottle opener had to be rotated slightly to match the angle of the opener lying on the floor. The layer was then given a Motion Blur filter in a vertical direction. Finally, the opacity for the layer was lowered to create a realistic reflection.

Next came the bottle's reflection. The bottle had to be created separately from the glass because of the position of the bottle in relation to the glass. If they were taken as a single unit, the glass would appear shorter than its actual size in the reflection. Creating a separate layer for the bottle made it easy to position it farther back from the reflection of the glass (Figure 78).

Details, like the lip of the glass and the label on the bottle, were not crucial because the reflection was to be heavily blurred.

Similar to the procedure of the video box reflection of the glory shot exercise, a copy was made of the front of the bottom crate (Figure 79). The layer with the copy was flipped vertically.

77 The wine glass and bottle opener were put into a layer. The layer was duplicated and flipped to create the reflection, and the Motion Blur filter was applied.

78 The layer for the reflection of the bottle was created separately from that of the glass to establish the proper position in relation to each other.

79 The front of the bottom crate was copied into a new layer.

Using the Skew function (Edit>Transform>Skew), the reflection was skewed to match the angle of the original crate above it (Figure 80).

The side of the bottom crate was also copied to its own layer. It was flipped vertically and then skewed to match the angle of the original side above it.

Preserve Transparency was turned on for this layer. With the Clone tool, I restored the far edge that was missing because it was obscured by the crate above it (Figure 81). This was necessary because this edge would be visible in the reflection.

80 The layer of the reflection of the crate was skewed to match the angle of the original.

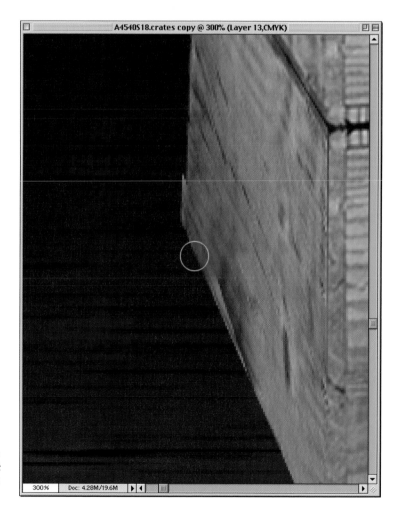

81 The side of the bottom crate was retouched to restore the edge that was hidden by the crate above it.

Because the angle of the crate is extreme, a little perspective had to be added to the reflection (Figure 82). With the Distort function (Edit>Transform>Distort), I made a slight alteration to the back edge.

The side of the top crate was copied to its own layer (Figure 83). Then the layer was flipped. The skew was greater than the actual edge because of added perspective, and the distortion of the back edge also was greater. This finished layer was then placed behind the layers of the bottom crate's reflection. The position was carefully arranged to match the overhang of the two crates in the original image.

82 The reflection needed some perspective added to create a realistic effect.

83 The side of the upper crate was copied to its own layer and then distorted to match the perspective for the overall scene.

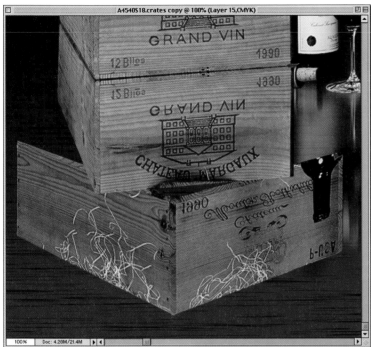

84 The front of the upper crate was put through the same paces as the sides of the other crates.

I followed the same procedure for the front of the upper crate (Figure 84).

Now came the extra touch needed for this type of reflection—the visible underside. The bottom of the crate on top should be visible in the reflection. With the Path tool, I created a path to simulate the bottom of the upper crate (Figure 85).

85 With the Path tool, a shape was created to simulate the bottom of the top crate.

217

The path was turned into a selection. A new layer was created behind the layers that made up the crates' reflection. The selection was filled with black (Figure 86).

With all the parts for the reflection of the crates complete, the layers were merged into a single layer. As with the other reflections, the crates' reflection was then blurred (Figure 87).

86 In a layer created to contain the bottom of the upper crate, the selection was filled with black.

87 The final reflections.

The Gallery:
Bert Looks Back

Welcome to the gallery section of the book. In these pages, I share with you some of my work that didn't make it to the body of the book. I want this gallery to serve as a sort of trip down the memory lane of digital art. I had a great time digging through mounds of disks to find some of this old stuff. I regret—well, maybe not totally—not having enough room for more. I took a little from here and a little from there and compiled stuff that relates to what I have covered in the book.

I eliminated any 3D files—and, of course, animation stuff is out of the question. One point I want to make is that you will find many similarities in subject matter and the way things are represented, but believe me, things are much easier today than they were. Tomorrow? Can't wait!

Let's start at the beginning. The digital beginning, that is. I did work with traditional media for decades before the Mac came along. I had a small ad agency at the time, and my partner said we had to computerize. I went down to my local computer store to see this Mac 128 thing. *Pow!* I found my medium! From that day back in 1984 on, I've been digital.

Back then there were only two programs for the "toy": MacWrite and MacPaint. I will admit I got into MacWrite. I could never read my writing, so word processing was very cool. MacPaint, on the other hand, was the tool I had been searching for!

MacPaint

MacPaint had some limitations. It was only black-and-white, 72 dpi, and eight by ten. The only printer was a dot-matrix Imagewriter. So who cared? Fatbits! That was the key for me. I was able to zoom in (1 level) and work on tiny details. This was a very exciting time. Everything was so new. There was so much promise of great things to come. I settled into a new lifestyle that involved little sleep and lots of Chinese food.

However, because of the limitations, I wasn't able to get the photorealistic effects that I can get today. While it was an exciting time, it was also a period of experimentation. All the images I created were from my imagination or memory. I want to start the gallery with a sampling of these explorations into the digital realm.

a door somewhere   —Bert Monroy '86

door somewhere 2.0

This image was an imaginary scene I conjured up. A little note: When HyperCard first came out, I took this image and turned it into a HyperCard stack. I assigned a link to every item. Each brick, for example, linked to something to do with bricks, like a scene of the building of the pyramids. I even had Pink Floyd singing "Just another brick in the wall."

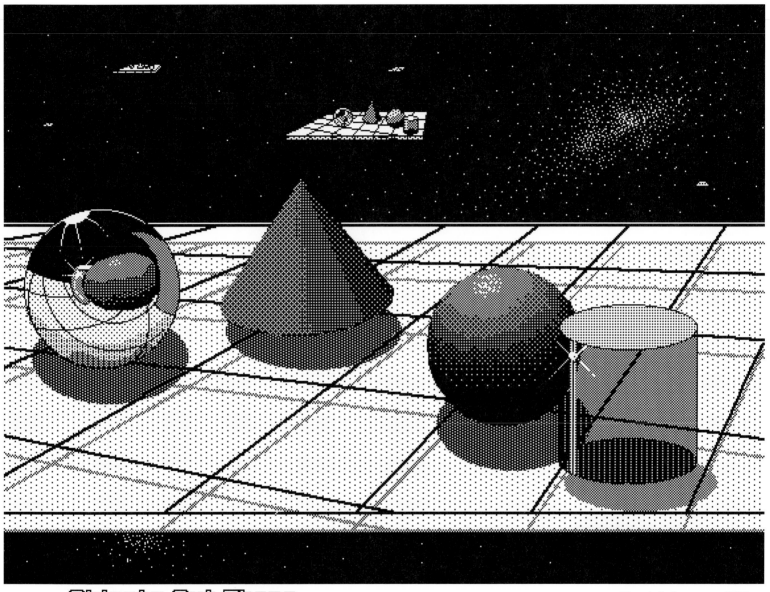

Objects Out There

-Bert Monroy '86

Objects Out There

I created this image for my friend, David. He wanted me to do something spacey. It was an exercise in reflection mapping. It wasn't perfect, but I had fun creating those reflections. This was my first digital art piece to be published in a national magazine. *MacUser* magazine had a gallery section, and this piece made it in.

Into It

This image was a statement on where I was
headed. I went a bit nuts on the reflections.

Reflection

Mark Zimmer and Tom Hedges (of Painter fame, not to mention a ton of other programs) had produced this cool little program called MacFractal. It generated mountains. The effects of MacFractal are what you see on the surface of the moon. This image also made it into a national magazine—*Verbum* magazine, the first of the digital art magazines. The editors gave me a lot of space through the years. It was a sad day when the magazine folded.

SoundCap

I created this early commercial illustration in MacPaint. Mark Zimmer and Tom Hedges put out this cool sound digitizer for the first Macs. This image was the cover for the manual. The letters are not from a 3D program, as there wasn't one available then.

The Shaver

Here is an example of the way inspiration can come from anywhere. My Gillette throwaway razor sat on a shelf in my shower when I saw this scene. It was painted from memory.

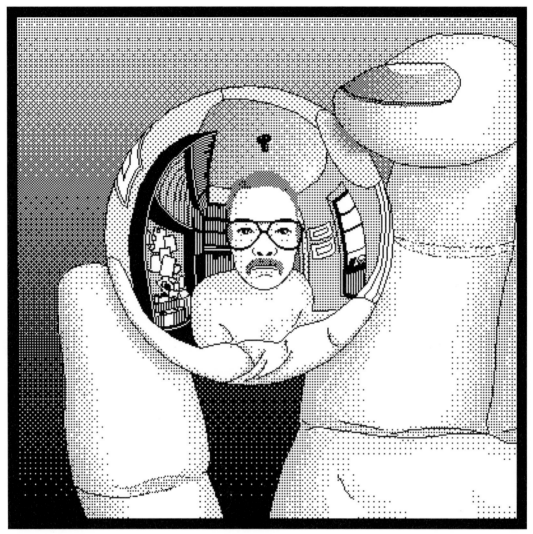

Dedicated to M.C.E.   —Bert Monroy '87

Dedicated to M.C.E.

This is the only image of the MacPaint work that was
done from life. It is my only self-portrait. I am sitting at
my desk, holding the cap from Polo, an aftershave bottle.

PixelPaint

When the Mac II was introduced, I thought I had died and arrived in heaven. Color on a Mac! The Apple IIs had color—but *this* was a Macintosh.

PixelPaint was one of the first color paint programs introduced after the debut of the Mac II. Two hundred fifty-six colors! What more could I want? Okay, so it, too, had limitations.

For one thing, it couldn't dither colors. To get smooth gradients, I had to use up large portions of the palette with the ramps of color. Let me try to explain this limitation. The image used the colors resident in the palette of 256 colors. When a gradient was created, each step of the gradient took a color space from the palette. Figure 1 shows the color palette for the image *street*. Figure 2 shows a close-up of the sky in the image, which has a gradient. Notice how many color swatches were dedicated in the palette to allow for the gradient.

Version 2.0 fixed that by creating a dither between steps of a gradient, so fewer colors were necessary. Let's say you needed a purple for your image but all the colors had already been assigned; the program took an existing red and blue and created a pixelated pattern of the two to simulate the desired purple. Figure 3 shows a close-up of a section of the sign in the painting *Dave's 5 & 10*. In this figure, you can see the dither created by mixing pixels of different colors. I was able to get a greater variety of colors into that 256-color palette, as is evident in Figure 4.

In defense of the color limitation of the PixelPaint program, let me point out that the maximum video RAM for the Mac II, at the time of PixelPaint's release, allowed for the display of only 256 colors.

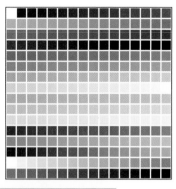

1 The color palette of PixelPaint was limited to 256 colors.

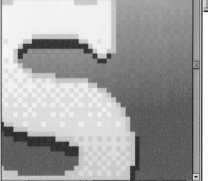

2 This close-up of the sky area of *street* shows the ramp of color from the palette. Note the banding as each color takes up a specific line of pixels.

3 This close-up of the sign in the image *Dave's 5 & 10* shows the dithering of colored pixels.

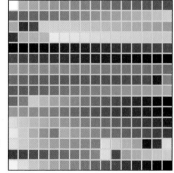

4 This is the palette for *Dave's 5 & 10*. Note how many more colors are available within the palette.

227

Florida

This image was one of the
first I created in PixelPaint.
It got tremendous circulation
at the time I created it. Not
much computer-generated art
done on a Mac was around
yet, and every company was
jumping on the color band-
wagon. Color printers were
arriving on the market, and
manufacturers were hungry
for samples so Florida was
turning up everywhere.

street

This image was created from my head. I was literally sitting in someone's closet when I started this painting. It was my first trip to San Francisco, and the person I was staying with kept the Mac in a walk-in closet. It was three in the morning and I couldn't sleep, so I started to paint an imaginary scene of some street in New York. No! I wasn't homesick. I just hadn't seen San Francisco yet. This image went on to win First Place for Illustration in *Macworld* magazine's first Macintosh Masters Art Contest, held in 1988.

Classic

PixelPaint finally had good gradients!

Moishe's Pippic

My first trip to San Francisco gave me tons of inspiration. This was one of the first images from that trip. A little sidenote: The overpasses visible down the street went away with the 1989 quake.

Falling Water

Falling Water was commissioned by *Macworld* magazine for a cover. They changed the cover story, and the painting ended up inside somewhere. The trees were done with an undocumented feature. In those days, Option+clicking with the Pencil tool would create fractal trees that were always different. The trees were in the foreground color. Option+Shift+click with the Pencil tool gave you trees that were the color of the foreground color and berries that were the color of the background color.

Blessing in Disguise

My good friend Walter commissioned this piece for one of the bands he managed. I used Illustrator 88 to create the shapes.

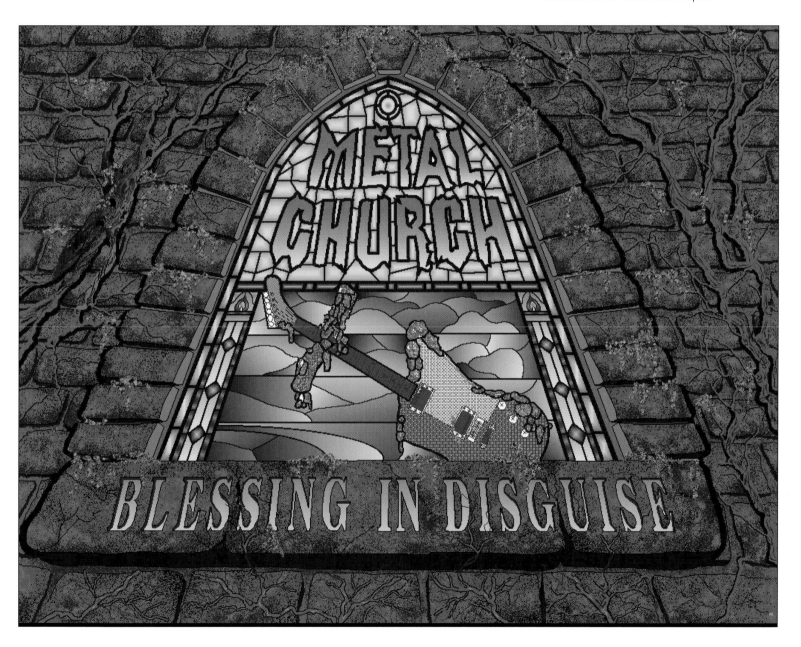

Dave's 5 & 10

This neighborhood fixture, around the corner from
where I lived, is still open in Brooklyn, New York.

Bert Monroy for McGraw-Hill 1988[N]

McGraw-Hill

This image was commissioned by McGraw-Hill in 1988 to be their corporate Christmas card. I used a feature of a new program at the time to create the building. Studio 8 had come on the scene as the first real competition for PixelPaint. It had a neat feature—you could select something and throw it into a perspective pattern.

The Subway Inn

Subway Inn is one of those places that's always been around and always will be. It's a dive of a place behind Bloomingdale's loading docks in Manhattan. When I was in high school, a few blocks away, this place was already old. This image was the first time I incorporated Photoshop into a painting. Photoshop was not yet commercially available, but it had a great Airbrush tool, which I used to create the dirt on the signs and walls.

236

PixelPaint Ad

SuperMac Technologies commissioned this piece to introduce PixelPaint Professional. Photoshop was entering the market at that point and would soon replace PixelPaint as the tool of choice. The technology was moving on.

Photoshop

When I first got Photoshop, I realized that there were no longer any limits. Things will only get better from now on—at least, in technology.

When Photoshop first came on the scene, the machines were not good enough for the programs. Photoshop could do all sorts of stuff, but the machines at the time were very slow. I laugh when I hear complaints of RAM and clock speeds today. One thing those days taught me is patience.

I have arranged the paintings in this section in as close to chronological order as I could.

Sphere chamber

I was experimenting with reflections. In case you hadn't noticed, I am fascinated with them. The concepts were identical to the ones I discuss in this book's chapters on reflections and shadows. The techniques were a little different back then, though.

Objects on cloth

An early Photoshop experiment in reflections and light refraction: Just a bunch of items hanging around the house.

Lock

More stuff around the house. There are times in New York when
the weather... well, let's just say it's hard to get out.

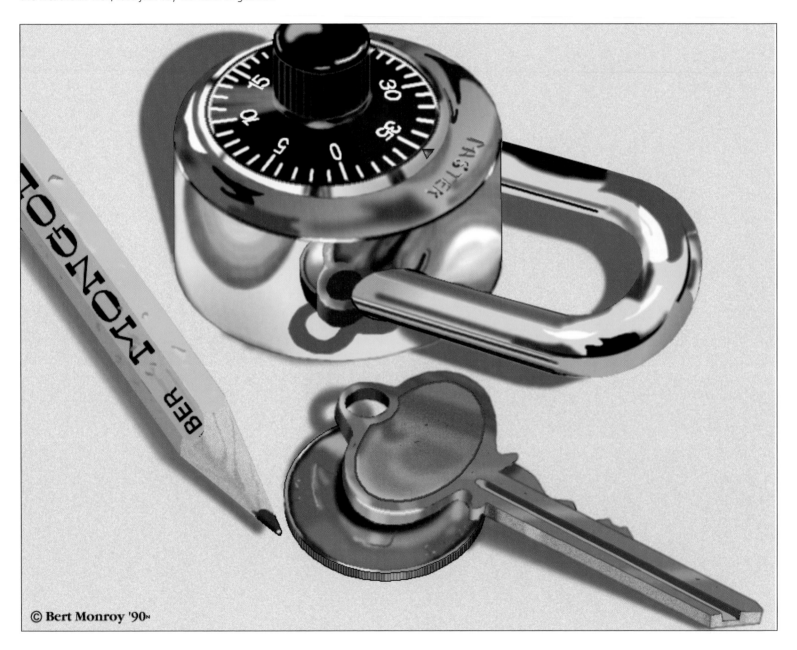

© Bert Monroy '90ℕ

Sam's

A great little restaurant in Brooklyn. Seventy-two dpi. Limited, but a long way from MacPaint.

© Bert Monroy '90

Height's Deli

What can I say? Brooklyn was a source for material.

Abraham Automotives

This was one of those places that jumped out at me and begged to be painted. We were on our way to the mountains outside Sydney, Australia, when I yelled out to stop the car so I could jump out and take a few shots of the place.

Parkers'

That's the Manhattan bridge in the background. Yep! You guessed it. We're back in Brooklyn.

© Bert Monroy 1992.

StuffIt bottle

This image was commissioned for an ad for the popular compression program. I put it in the gallery for my friend, David S.

Altoids

It was the El Ninõ year—raining every day. Whenever I paint a still life, it's a good bet I'm stuck at home.

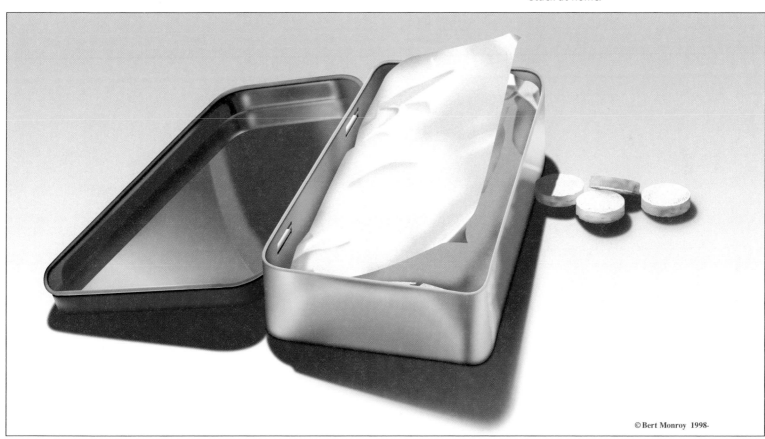

© Bert Monroy 1998·

Window in Krakow

This window caught my attention on a recent trip to Poland. The sun
hit it in such a way that it told me many stories of the past.

Index

INCREASE YOUR PHOTOSHOP IQ TODAY!

"I steal my best ideas from David Biedny"
Russell Brown, Senior Creative Director at Adobe Systems, and Adobe's In-House Photoshop Genius

"See Photoshop as you've never seen it before!"
Computer Arts, Britain's biggest-selling creative magazine

From the minds of David Biedny and Bert Monroy - coauthors of several books on Photoshop (including the bestselling "The Official Adobe Photoshop Handbook", the *first* book on Photoshop ever, and "Photoshop Channel Chops", the most advanced Photoshop book on the market), two of the original innovators in the field of computer education, and two of the earliest proponents of computer-based multimedia for corporate applications - comes a new type of video-based learning series, Photoshop Inside & Out. Advanced video production technology and computer visualizations are used in ways that few - if any - instructors have ever attempted. FORGET THE REST, LEARN FROM THE BEST!

The Photoshop Inside & Out series will appeal to *anyone* working with Photoshop

Welcome to Photoshop 5.0 - Parts 1 & 2	Photoshop for the Web
Optimum Scanning Techniques	Photoshop Fundamentals
Photoshop Power User Tips & Tricks	Alpha Channels & Masking
Layers & Image Compositing	Calculations & Advanced Channel Techniques
Illustrating With Photoshop - Parts 1 & 2	Special Effects with Photoshop
Lost in Color Space	CMYK/Prepress Tips & Tricks

Now you can have David and Bert (and their friends!) at your side when you need them the most - when you're trying to get work done on time, in the smartest way possible. Once you've experienced Photoshop Inside & Out, you'll never need another videotape learning series again! Order today, and learn from the Masters of Photoshop.

Also available in PAL (European format).

www.photoshopio.com

IDIG, Inc.

P.O. Box 151498 • San Rafael, CA 94915 • USA
Sales: 1-877-4-IDIGPS (1-877-443-4477)
International Sales: +1-415-460-6889
sales@photoshopio.com

[Deep Knowledge *for* Everyone.]™

New Riders Professional Library

Colophon

Bert Monroy: Photorealistic Techniques with Photoshop & Illustrator was layed out and produced with the help of Microsoft Word, Adobe Photoshop, Adobe Illustrator, and QuarkXPress on a variety of systems, including a Macintosh G3. With the exception of the pages that were printed out for proofreading, all files—both text and images—were transferred via email or ftp and edited on-screen.

All the body text and headings were set in the Rotis Serif family. All figure captions and cover text were set in the Rotis Sans Serif family. Zapf Dingbats and Symbol were used throughout for special symbols and bullets.

This book was printed on 70# Courtland Matte at GAC (Graphic Arts Center) in Indianapolis, Indiana. Prepress consisted of PostScript computer-to-plate technology (filmless process). The cover was printed on 12-pt. Frankote, coated on one side.

Dedication

...for Z.